Keeping time

Edited by

MARY AZRAEL & **KENDRA KOPELKE**

150 years of journal writing

Publisher's Cataloging-In-Publication Data
(Prepared by The Donohue Group, Inc.)
 Keeping time : 150 years of journal writing / Mary Azrael and Kendra Kopelke, editors.
    p. : ill. ; cm.
   A collection of excerpts from personal journals
collected over a period of two years from contributors
and subscribers to the literary journal "Passager."
   ISBN: 978-09631385-4-5
1. Diaries--Authorship. 2. Older people's writings. I. Azrael, Mary.
II. Kopelke, Kendra. III. Title: Passager :
a journal of remembrance and discovery.
PN4390.K44 2009
808.883 2009929417

Passager Books is in residence at the University of Baltimore
in the School of Communications Design.
PASSAGER BOOKS
1420 North Charles Street
Baltimore, Maryland 21201
www.passagerpress.com

A diary means yes indeed.

And now.

Today today is celebrated in our annals by perfect satisfaction.

Gertrude Stein

Dedicated to the power of the pen,
the keyboard, the pencil, the ink,

the camera, the brush,
the notebook, the letters,

the commas, the cross-outs,
the dashes, the truths, the typos, the

bewilderments, the insights,
the memories,

the surprises . . .

Contents

Contents

Contents

Contents

Introduction

A few years ago *Passager* magazine put out a call to our readers for excerpts from their journals, diaries, or artist notebooks. For many people, journal writing is a private activity, spontaneous and revealing, not intended for an audience of strangers. We wondered whether anyone would be willing to submit such personal work. Journal keepers ourselves, and voracious readers of other people's journals, we were curious about what we would find among our community of readers and writers.

The very first submission was unexpectedly poignant. A poet we had previously published in *Passager* sent us part of his visual journal – twelve small watercolors, one for each month of the year following his wife's death. He said in his letter that keeping this journal was enormously helpful to him during this difficult time.

There were other surprises: someone sent us excerpts from a 100-year-old diary she had found at a flea market. She had photocopied the actual pages from the journal so we could see the faded handwriting, and when she typed them, she used the same line breaks and page breaks (something we wouldn't have thought to do ourselves), to keep the reading experience as close to the original as possible. The effect of this exact transcription was that the diary read with the intensity and compression of a poem.

Another sent journal excerpts from four generations of women in her family, including her 9-year-old daughter. Another, after her mother died, discovered journals she had kept in the last years of her life and found, in those notebooks, "the mother [she] hadn't had in life." An Israeli hiding from SCUD missiles managed to keep her journal throughout the war. A passenger on a grounded flight on September 11 described her life-changing experience. A photographer sent 75 photos (she took 2800) of pigeons hatching in a flowerpot on the balcony of her urban condominium.

We chose 37 pieces that moved us and added to the infinite variety of approaches to journal writing. Then began the challenge of making a book of these disparate subjects, sensibilities, writing styles and time periods. We thought of categories: historical events, everyday life, parents, children, nature, travel. But ultimately we found that when we read them chronologically, from 1867 to 2008, these personal stories brought "History" to life as a fascinating, vibrant story told by many voices.

Small decisions loomed large. Should we correct spelling and punctuation mistakes? Add missing words? How faithful should we be to the original? The more involved we got, the more important it was for us to preserve *everything* – the handwriting or typing, scratch-outs, punctuation, headings, decorations.

All of these elements contribute to the story the writer tells, whether or not we as readers are able to discover the significance.

You may notice the ways in which journal keeping has changed over the years, down to the tools we have to write with, and the ways technology influences how we express ourselves. (Compare the spareness of a 19th century handwritten diary to the sheer volume – 2,400,000 words in 7 years – generated by a writer on his laptop.) But in all times and places, whether handwritten or typed, painted or photographed, the journal expresses a fundamental human impulse. As Diana Anhalt explains in the introduction to her pages:

When I don't keep a journal, life rushes by like the view from a train window, events smudge, become grainy. But when I do, I find myself focusing on what's going on around me. Once something is in writing, I tell myself, it's less likely to disappear.

Keeping Time stands as witness to the times spanning from our great grandparents to today. It opens a way into our history at its most intimately and sincerely felt, and expands our sense of what a notebook can do to connect us more fully to our lives.

What's Forgotten

Walking alone through a Taipei park, I came across what looked to be a writer's notebook wedged in the crotch of this tree. I could only guess it had slipped out of the poet's pocket without him noticing and someone picked it up from the path and stuck it in the tree so it wouldn't get trampled and ruined. Would the writer remember to come back to this place to look? I didn't even think to steal a look at someone's private words but took this photo and emailed it to an American poet I knew in Taipei who used the same kind

of notebook. He wrote back it wasn't one of his. I left for Taichung the following day.

Late one evening many years ago I sat alone in my New York apartment to watch a movie I'd rented about the life of a great British writer. Midway through the story the man said to his students a few words so filled with truth and beauty that they cut me to the quick. I reached for the remote, switched off the movie and sat there in the dark for a few sad moments. For years I'd been waking up early every morning to write in my journal, but to hear such profound words from the mouth of that great man made me realize I didn't have it in me to be a writer. I recognized how pitiful it was that I'd tried so hard at writing for so many years when I had no talent.

I couldn't imagine what had ever made me think I could do it to begin with. I got up and went to the bathroom, then came back and started the tape again to watch the rest of the movie. Afterwards I went right to bed.

In the morning I woke and went to my desk. I wrote about the episode and my realization. Then, as was my habit after the morning writing, I went back to read the entry I'd made on the same day the previous year. Imagine my surprise to find I'd had an experience that day that had brought me to exactly the same insight the writer had expressed in the film – only in my journal entry I said it better.

Should it come as any surprise that every single one of us has inside the same greatness? Or that, like the notebook in the park, this so easily gets mislaid and then forgotten? When we are touched by the deep truth of a writer's words, we recognize greatness. It makes us feel small. Because we've forgotten the greatness is our own. ♣

William Stinson

1867

The Diary of William Easterly and Margaret P. Wilson Van Slyke

This journal was kept by my paternal great grandparents, Margaret (Maggie) P. and William (Will) E. Van Slyke, during the first two years of their marriage. The diary was written in pencil and is very faded. Maggie's entries are written at the bottom of pages where Will had made entries in 1866.

I have selected a portion written by Maggie documenting the first week of her reunion with her husband after more than a year of separation early in their marriage. At that time, they were traveling in a wagon train between Julesburgh (near the present day borders of Nebraska and Colorado) and Salt Lake City.

This section of the journal touches on Maggie's youth, vulnerability and her spirit of adventure, as well as her devotion to her new husband. The final entry shows her religious convictions, which I imagine are typical of a young Mormon woman of her time.

Vicki Broadrick

SATURDAY, JULY 6

Arrived at Julesburgh
met my Dear Husband was
rejoiced to be with him once
again only think how have I
lived a year four months and
five days with out him – lonely
and unhappy but the joy of
meeting the rest and peace of
being with him again dri-
ves in to oblivion the un
happy past May God bless us
and make us happy henceforth

MONDAY, JULY 8

Will went to the Station
I washed my first washing
for Will. I think it a funny
way to live out doors
who would have thought it
washing cooking outdoors
eating in a tent sleeping
in a wagon yet happy
Oh well such is woman
Beloved and Loving her life

TUESDAY, JULY 9

warm at noon
windy at night, we
eat drink and sleep
endure still happy
Will and I. He sais I
may go back will I
shall I. Could I.
no no. never while we
live must we separate
again Husband and wife
one flesh. "Leave Father
Mother and cleave to your
husband" is the words of our
[continues up the binding side ways] devine Lord Very Pamesn[?]

WEDNESDAY, JULY 10

As usual warm and
cool Also windy our
encampment is plea
ent the river makes
it pleasant I like to
wander down along its
banks Will is in
town wish he would

come back, for I am
lonly when he goes away
returned all right held
in his arms all night

THURSDAY, JULY 11

Cool morning warm
sultry noon cool and
chilly night. Will in town all day
went back at night
we took dinner with Mrs.
C. had a good dinner Will
stayed so long I got tired
went to bed felt ugly when
he returned acted like a child
instead of a woman

FRIDAY, JULY 12

washed and made
pudding for dinner
it is very warm a great
many mosquitos arond
bite like everything
Oh Dear how the wind
blows make me think

I would like to say Good
bye to life I hate the wind
cannot sleep Will mules
has run away he feels badly

SATURDAY, JULY 13

Mules found Will feels
better I also Will the
winds blows. We leave our
encampment for another
near Julesburgh Rode
in my new wagon found
it very comfortable. It is
as nice as can be Will
is a dear Good Hubby. We
have a little rain. I have
a little homesick feeling
but like the [along binding]
rain did not amount to much

SUNDAY, JULY 14

Sunday Dull and
cool yet a quiet prevails
which breathes of the Holy
Sabbath day. How differ-

ent from all other days
is the Sabbath even here
so far from civilization
must the voice of God
be heard. Remember the Sab
bath + keep it Holy yet
how prone are we to forget it
If God would let us but the
rest and peace which entrs
into the inmost soul on this
day breath of the infinite
One. and we can not but feel
that this day is Thine O Lord
each us to Honor it above
all other days. ♣

1900

Ella Fisher's Diary

A couple of years ago, I bought a little 1900 diary at an antique store for $12. I was intrigued by the daily life recorded by this (then) anonymous woman, and also by her vivid use of language. I had only the first names of her husband and children to go by, so it took a bit of detective work – 1900 Vermont Census, online – to discover her name: Ella Fisher. I also poked through records at the Vergennes City Clerk's Office and learned a bit more about her and her family. (There were eight children altogether.) Finally, I managed to locate the widow of Ella's grandson Warner, Yvette Field, who loaned me one of the five books of poetry that Ella Warner Fisher had published in her lifetime. A blurb on the jacket of the book, published in North Montpelier, Vermont, said that she had been referred to as "our beloved dean of women poets." It goes on to say, "She is not an obscurantist; nor is she a vivisectionist of emotion." Ella Warner Fisher lived to be 84. Visiting the family gravesite and seeing those familiar names on tombstones was quite a moving experience, as was returning the diary to the family.

Mary Pratt

JANUARY

Once more I'll start in to keep a diary and hope it won't be half blank.
Once more the pages of the New Year are clean and white.

Make bread, 5 mince pies & doughnuts.
Mop. Bathe children.
Squeeze out tallow, boil mincemeat.
Commence a skirt for Grace.
Mend Henry's cap, (etc) in the evening.

To day I am 47.
I want to look forward with pleasure
to the home He has prepared to which I am one year nearer.
[It] looks a long way, and I am on the last half of the journey.
Finish Anna's dress.
Helen gives me 3 cakes of nice soap.
Clean out sitting room, parlor & hall.
Read the children a story in the evening.

Wind blows a blizzard after noon.
No one attends evening service.
Stormed all night, plough comes up so we get out.
Children go to school in the morning but come home at noon through the storm.

Make bread.

Lay down in the evening.

Guess I am about sick.

A bright day. Snow piled in drifts very cold.

Helen & I drive out to Robinson's –

have a delightful afternoon though very short.

Almost frozen & go early to bed.

A dark day. Sew a little. Sweep 2 chambers.

Rain in the evening.

Rain freezes to everything it touches:

the whole world, so far as I can see, is a glade of ice.

My umbrella frozen together tears itself to peices {sic} when I raise it.

[We] wash & mop and at [night] the clothes are piled in a big chair,

stark as so many ghosts.

APRIL

Feel very miserable after dinner & lie down most of the afternoon.

Cut out Grace a shirt waist.

Henry tears up sitting room

& takes out the jog on the chimney.

A large wash.
Merrill comes at noon
& they commence laying the sitting room floor.
Clean dining room closet
& put away the stove in the evening.

They finish laying the sitting room floor.
We iron.

Henry plasters in sitting room (pantry) & bedroom.
I clean up plaster.
Make custard pies A.M.
Mend a little &ct.
Grace & Mrs. Aiken baptized after Prayer Meeting.

Mend A.M.
Attend Mission Circle P.M.
Prepare the program.
Topic on the [Freedman]
12 ladies present.

Children go to the farm for milk.
Henry goes to the Lake.

The old cow has a calf
& we shall have milk soon.

Attend church.
Attend church.
Attend church.
Attend church.

AUGUST

A fearful hot day.
A severe storm at night with high wind,
doing much damage & sharp lightning.
Strikes Jasper Bostwick's house & barns:
burns up; no insurance.

Showery.
Have sick headache & lie abed, so nothing is done.
Grace attending teachers exams.

Benjamin sticks a needle into his leg out of sight.
Dr. Gibson cuts it open takes out the needle & sews up the gash.

Cool & beautiful.

After dinner we all go to Ben's.
Jim falls down & breaks the shaft
on the new buggay in front of Den Woodman's.
They help us out & lend us their carriage.
Some frightened but no one is hurt.

Go down & spend the afternoon with Hattie.
Gertrude goes to the station to meet Ruth and carries me home.
I meet Helena at the 3 P.M. train.

Wash, mop &ct. & some other things.
Finish ironing, mend, &ct.
A hot day.
Maud sings to us in the evening.

Andrew & family, Addie & I
go to Lake Dunmore & have a delightful time.
Visit the Cascades & Ethan Allen's cave.
Get home just at dark.
A lovely day long to be remembered.

Benjamin gone to Burlington
but comes home today with his father & full of the fair.

DECEMBER

Henry kills the pigs.
Mother carries Grace to her school.
Go down to Mr. Bartlett's to teachers meeting.
Sort meat.
Cut up lard & grind sausages.

Mix sausage & bag 1/2 of it.
Clean head & put it cooking.
Finish lard.
Wash all day.
Make head cheese &ct.
Attend prayer meeting in the evening.
Henry goes to Burlington P.M. & back on the last train.
Mother finishes the sausage.

Work all day about the house.
Finish the meat business.
Henry goes after Grace.
She was sick yesterday & could not teach school.
Mend in the evening.

Make pumpkin pies, bathe children.
Attend to the S. S. lesson.
Sick tonight & hurry off to bed.

Storming & blowing. Very cold.
Wind goes through the house like a seive. {sic}
School closes for two weeks.

Attend church. Rehearsal takes the place of the S. S.
Write Xmas letters until late.

Tuttle goes to Montpelier & takes dinner with his father,
we have a plain dinner of baked beans & brown bread.
Grace & Helen help at the church P.M.
In the evening we all attend the tree, 7 of us.
My class gives me a lovely birthday book. ♣

1919

Joseph Levy's Travel Diary: Smyrna to New York

My father, Joseph Levy, emigrated to New York from Izmir, Turkey – then known as Smyrna – in December of 1919 when he was 19 or 20 years old. His eldest brother was already married and in New York. The voyage on a Greek ship, the SS *Themistokles*, took six weeks and he traveled in third class, not steerage, as he was proud of saying. Nonetheless, conditions were poor, and the food was often inedible. Much of his travel diary is devoted to what he ate or couldn't eat.

The diary is written in pencil in French, which he learned, like other Sephardic boys, at the local Alliance Israélite Universelle school. These schools were founded by Jews in France who were concerned about the cultural backwardness of their co-religionists in the Ottoman Empire. Despite some misspellings, my father frequently uses elegant turns of phrase, like subjunctives, and the past definite tense which, coming from a person who never had much schooling, are surprising.

I've translated the following excerpts into English.

Gloria DeVidas Kirchheimer

THURSDAY, OCTOBER 23

I left home on Thursday morning at 8:30. The separation was very emotional. First my sister kissed me and hugged me so hard I was afraid of suffocating. After embracing me she left for work sobbing, her eyes red. Then my father hugged me so hard that the hairs of his moustache and his beard pierced my cheeks, but I would have wished that pain to remain forever as a constant reminder of him. When it was my mother's turn, I hardly had the energy to kiss her, I was so overwhelmed, and trembled with emotion. She made me promise to take care of myself and to never do anything frivolous.

I will keep my word to follow her advice. With Isaac and Leon [his brothers] I made a superhuman effort and didn't cry. I embraced them and promised to send for them from New York, along with our parents, as soon as possible.

FRIDAY, OCTOBER 24

At 10:00 my ship SS *Themistoklis* prepared for departure. A ship dropped anchor next to us, full of Greek soldiers singing their heads off. Gradually, the dock filled with people waiting to see our ship leave. Promptly at noon, it raised anchor. I kept seeing the dock and the whole city. I wanted to be sure to absorb this sight because God knows if I'll ever see the dear city of my birth again. . . .

Thank God the sea has been calm. I was introduced to a passenger named Max Mahlers. He's originally from Poland but has been living in America for a

long time in the city of Philadelphia, an hour and a half from New York.
He only knows English so for me it's a very good opportunity. That's
all we speak together. I hope to make substantial progress by the time
we arrive in New York.

MONDAY, OCTOBER 27

. . . I slept in a cabin with the Sayegh family. Since there was no blanket
I went to bed half dressed and used my overcoat as a cover. The next day,
Tuesday the 28th, I went down to see the third-class quarters where I was
going to be sleeping. I found it so dark that I was miserable and almost cried.

[The ship docked in Piraeus. Passengers were required to leave the ship in
order to be vaccinated and to have their luggage disinfected. The ship would
also be disinfected and passengers were to spend the night on shore in a hotel.]

THURSDAY, OCTOBER 29

Once again we had to see the doctor, with the American consul present.
There were so many people jostling each other in order to get in more quickly
that I was reminded of the time when fights broke out in Smyrna when we
tried to get bread, during the war [WWI]. . . .

Adjacent to our ship is another one manned by black Hindus. These
people wear only pants and sleeveless shirts. Some were just wearing pants.
They eat with their hands and never eat bread. It was very funny to see them
eat. They make a little stack of food and put it into their mouths. They also

don't sit down. They eat bent over their plates. When they finished eating they washed their hands and teeth with soap. Others soaped their entire bodies, outdoors. Some of us felt chilly just watching them.

WEDNESDAY, NOVEMBER 4

. . . They served rice with meat that wasn't well cooked, and the rice was mixed with bits of wood. . . . I stayed up on deck until 11:00. We had fun dancing Turkish, French and Greek style, playing violin and mandolin, but everything got spoiled. While we were having a good time a mechanic came out of his cabin in a rage, saying that we were only allowed on deck until 8:00 and we had to leave because we were preventing him from sleeping. The first and second-class passengers were upset by his manner, and . . . complained to his superior who came and told us we could continue, but to go a little further away so the others could sleep.

THURSDAY, NOVEMBER 6

At the port of Gibraltar I was able to count at least 100 boats. We were allowed to buy things brought by the Spanish boats. They were selling oranges, grapes, pomegranates and apples. In order to sell them, the boatmen threw a rope which we secured, and at the other end they attached a basket. We first put the money in and then they sent up our purchases. It was really funny to watch them cast up the ropes while cursing. First they didn't want to accept Greek money but they finally gave in. They preferred dollars.

MONDAY, NOVEMBER 10

. . . Today we're very dirty because we're taking on coal and the dust penetrates our bodies [*organes*] . . . Our beds were as black as coal. All the dust had piled up and the pillows especially were as dark as coal. We dusted them off and turned the mattresses around, and then we went to bed after giving ourselves a good wash.

TUESDAY, NOVEMBER 11

I got up as dirty as though I'd been in a coal heap.

FRIDAY, NOVEMBER 14

We sent a petition to the captain complaining about the dirtiness of our beds and the bad food. He ordered the sleeping area to be cleaned and had them serve us a good meal at noon. . . . They won't let us get off the ship at Gibraltar because we're in 3rd class.

TUESDAY, NOVEMBER 18

I'm suffering terribly with my tooth. I've gone four times to look for the doctor so he can extract the tooth. I also feel very weak. What I wanted to eat was a good soup, and luckily, that's what they served along with some meat. I ate like a famished person. I hadn't eaten for a day and a half. But after I was done, the toothache started up with a vengeance. I was like a crazy man. When the doctor finally arrived he told me that the dentist was a woman passenger who would take out my tooth. . . . She finally came. I went to the pharmacy with her and I myself gave her the cotton to use while they looked for a chair for me. First she cleaned the molar and prepared a spot where she could grasp the tooth with the pincers, since the tooth was so decayed.

After three attempts she pulled it out. The second time, it felt as though my jaw was being wrenched. After she pulled the tooth I cried out – *Maman* – and then choked up with sobs. I cried a little. I wanted to cry some more but I was ashamed. I started to faint and they made me inhale some ether. . . .

THURSDAY, DECEMBER 4

. . . At 9 o'clock, my friend Salomon came to fetch me and found me still in bed. He said the ship was due to arrive in New York at 11:00. I got up to see this with my own eyes and it was true. . . . People were calling and yelling and on top of that it was freezing cold, our hands were numb. . . .

As we got closer the harbor pilot boarded in order to guide us in, planes were flying overhead. We saw a submarine pass, a barge with train cars. And finally, what I most wanted to see, the Statue of Liberty.

Then we saw what they said was the tallest building in New York, 54 stories, and at a distance, the Brooklyn Bridge. They cast anchor at 3:00. . . . The doctor came and made us file in front of him. Then he went to examine the 1st and 2nd class passengers and the crew. He didn't have time for us and so they left us for the following day.

There was a crowd of people on shore. I told myself that my brother was surely there. Passengers were calling out to those on shore. People were recognizing each other from a distance, shouting greetings, and lots of questions.

Unfortunately, after calling out my brother's name many times, I got no answer. So I went below to eat. When I was in the middle of cutting an onion which I was going to eat with some string beans, I heard my name called. Right away I rushed to the door. I was told that my brother was calling me on the other side of the ship.

I was rushing so, that I fell down and injured my knees. I continued running while limping. When I got there, I was exhausted. I yelled at the top of my lungs, "Elie!" Immediately I heard my name called by my brother but I didn't recognize his voice. He asked me how Papa was, and how I was, and whether I had an overcoat. His voice was unrecognizable. He also told me that someone would meet me if he was unable to do so. After we waved to each other, I went back down to finish eating. The beans were very tough. . . . ♣

town and with no employment possibilities, ~~interest in~~ a USNavy
career seemed a logical solution, ~~which~~ view was shared by brother
Herman (who just returned home) and neighbor Ralph Niccum (unemploye
since we graduated from the 8th grade) and ~~on~~ 10 March we reported
to Fargo, N.D. Recruiting Station. No vacancies existed and rather
than return home Herman and Ralph decided (we) should join the USArm
and though I objected they won me over and we proceeded to Minneapol
for finalization of enlistment.

Arriving in Minneapolis we initially proceeded to Concordia Colleg
St. Paul to see brother Ben only to promptly land in Pres. Graebner'
office who took a dim view of us, our mission to see our brother, th
USArmy and everything else but finally agreed we could visit for 10
minutes. We then found he was a diptheria patient, St. Paul Hospita
so we headed for the Recruiting Office at Fort Snelling where we
were examined, tested, lectured and sworn into the Service for three
years at $21.00 a month and emoluments.

The nightmare was on, being thrown in with other new enlistees,
mostly loud-mouthed city slickers who had little respect for themselves or others, predominantly a thieving, lying, double-crossing
conglomeration and it was only the dread fear of consequences that
kept me from deserting the hideous inhospitable barracks, the ███
food (subsistance ration was 18 ¢ a day); the profane dictatorial
drill instructors directing our every move from proper bed-making
to scrubbing and painting quarters, doing kitchen police (I peeled
small soft sprouted potatoes my entire first day under hazards of a
a half-drunk cook throwing butcher knives at us (always scoring near
misses); raked, scraped and policed the area; reported to the Servic
Company for a team of mules and wagon with which we hand-shovelled
and hauled coal to various designated barracks; polished the black
buttons on our WWI uniforms until the underlying brass surfaced;
re-colored bright YELLOW service shoes into dark brown ones (accomplished by saturating shoe with dyanshine, then 'burning' the sho
surface until the desired hue was obtained) all the while being directed to purchase various items of uniform equipment such as orname
insignia and the like. (As I recall the disagreeableness of everything military during those two weeks, ███████ t nowhere could one
find a cleaner, more spotless environment simply because all men whe
not on a specific work detail were cleaning, scrubbing, painting,
polishing the entire barracks and all its appurtances within & withc

Too soon we again were on the mule/wagon coal detail and returning
that evening to the stables we passed directly by the Reveille/Retre
cannon and knew it was due to be fired so we decided to test the

1925

Colonel Bill Hoffmann's Journal

We were an Army family until Colonel Bill, my dad, retired in 1956. When he was in his early 90s, he came and lived with me in the northwoods where I was working in a sawmill. I quit the mill in 2000 and cared for him until he passed away in 2002 at the age of 96, relatively healthy, when he didn't survive a broken hip repair.

Dad wrote this while in the service and, apparently, rewrote it in the early seventies. I found the typed journal in his records, in poor shape. It begins in 1925 and continues through his retirement.

William C. Hoffmann

1925

Father having disposed of the small farm adjacent to our place in town, and with no employment possibilities, a U.S. Navy career seemed a logical solution. This view was shared by Brother Herman and a neighbor, Ralph Niccum (unemployed since we graduated from the eighth grade). We reported to the Fargo ND Naval recruiting station on 10 March to discover no vacancies existed. Herman and Ralph then decided that we should join the Army. They won me over and we proceeded to Fort Snelling where we were examined, tested, lectured, and sworn into the Service for three years at $21 a month and emoluments.

The nightmare began: thrown in with other new enlistees, mostly loud-mouthed city slickers, who had little respect for themselves or others; who were predominantly a thieving, lying, double-crossing conglomeration. It was only the dread fear of consequences that kept me from deserting the hideous, inhospitable barracks. The food was terrible (subsistence ration was 18 cents a day) and the profane, dictatorial drill instructors directed our every move from proper bed-making to scrubbing and painting quarters and doing kitchen police. (My first day of KP, I peeled small, soft, sprouted potatoes under hazard of a half-drunk cook throwing butcher knives at the wall above me – scoring near misses!)

We raked, scraped and policed the area. I reported to the Service Company for a team of mules and a wagon with which we hand shoveled and hauled coal to designated barracks.

We polished the black buttons on our WWI uniforms until the underlying brass surfaced, and re-colored bright YELLOW service shoes into dark brown ones – this accomplished by saturating shoe with dyanshine, then burning the shoe surface until the desired hue was obtained. Though I recall the disagreeableness of everything military those first two weeks, nowhere could one find a cleaner, more spotless environment, simply because all men who were not on a specific work detail were cleaning, scrubbing, painting, and polishing the entire barracks and all its appurtenances within and without. . . .

Too soon we were again on the mule/wagon coal detail and returning that evening to the stables we passed directly by the Reveille/Retreat cannon. Knowing it was due to be fired, we decided to test the mule's reaction to cannon fire. The gun boomed without a flicker of concern on the mule's part. However, a Madman rushed to the wagon ordering the three of us to dismount, screaming invectives, demanding names and serial numbers! Why in hell had we not dismounted and saluted when the gun was fired? He finally realized we were "recruits" and with a blistering, profane tongue-lashing, he direly predicted "real" military men would haunt us forever and rightfully so.

A word concerning the two barracks bags of personal clothing and equipment issued to us. They contained woolen, high collar uniforms complete with dismal spiral leggings, bright yellow shoes, hats, caps, overcoats, rain coats, toilet articles including a "housewife" (sewing kit); also footwear, tent equipment, a complete rifle with bayonet, ammo belts and a pair of skis! Most clothing and equipment required tailoring and/or immediate attention at one's own expense and time, which also took a huge bite of the monthly stipend of $21.

On two occasions we were lectured on general military subjects by Sgt. John R. Watt, our acting First Sergeant. It was not only what he said but his entire personality that brightened our day. He was an intelligent individual of excellent military bearing and appearance with an outstanding WWI record even though still in his twenties. He was considerate, forceful and, to a man, respected but feared, he being an exact opposite of the bumbling, profane, not too intelligent instructors who regularly berated us.

What was further intriguing, we had the only First Sgt. in the U.S. Army who was rearing his three month old daughter in his private room in the Barracks – his wife having died in childbirth. I recall a newspaper which reported "a hard-boiled First Sergeant was lecturing his troops when suddenly a plaintive cry was heard from the barracks – whereupon the Sergeant turned the troops over to a subordinate, disappearing to attend to the child's needs." The situation evoked wide publicity resulting in many adoption offers which were initially rejected by Sgt. Watt. Finally realizing the difficulties involved in rearing a child in an inhospitable barracks room, Major and Mrs. Wainer adopted the child. They provided an excellent home for the girl. ♣

1950

The Saga of Our Passport

I am a professional pianist and piano teacher. I started writing late in life. My father's death triggered me to write, mostly because he was such a marvelous storyteller and I wanted to preserve his stories for future generations. But that wasn't simple. As a Romanian born, this was my first language, French was second. After immigrating to Israel in 1958 I learned Hebrew. Finally after coming to the United States, at age 33, I learned English from my piano students.

From 1977 to 1980 I wrote memoirs. A hiatus of 20 years followed while I pursued my musical career. In 2000 I moved to Florida where I joined a group of writers and my love for writing was rekindled. Many of my stories tell about life in Romania during WWII and under the Communist regime. Other stories deal with a new immigrant's life in Israel, and finally the experiences encountered as a "greener" in the United States.

I dedicate the publishing of my diary's excerpts to my mother's memory. She passed away a year ago, at the age of 95.

Fedora Horowitz

APRIL 2

This morning the mailman brought us the awaited postcard from The Office of the Secretary of Interior Affairs. Imprinted on it was a single word APROBAT (approved). My parents hugged me with tearing eyes. "We are going to Israel," my father whispered rubbing his hands, a sign of great excitement, while my mother put a finger on her lips. "Don't tell nobody."

I know she's afraid of the evil eye.

APRIL 3

Last night my father sang the most beautiful Passover Seder and when he got to the end, "next year we should celebrate in Jerusalem," I thought that the thousand year dream of the Diaspora Jews to return to the Holy Land is going to become reality for us. Next Passover we'll celebrate in Jerusalem!

APRIL 4

My father just returned from the Department of Interior. With new wrinkles on his forehead he told us about the documents he has to gather in order to receive our passports. Besides our birth certificates and my parents' marriage license, he has to bring a letter from the Department of Treasury stating that we don't owe any taxes. "Also," he added, "since our apartment has been nationalized, we need a letter from the Department of Housing confirming that we will leave the apartment in perfect condition. This means we'll have to paint, clean the parquet floors, windows, basement, the full works." Our passports are valid for three months only, expiring on July 1st.

APRIL 14

My mother is too busy. When I want to talk to her, she says, "Go practice your piano. You know we won't be able to take it to Israel and God knows when we'll have enough money to buy you another one."

APRIL 15

We have to sell an entire household in order to reduce our belongings to the 70 pounds the government allows each person to take out of the country. Now we have to get rid of things it took my parents 20 years to accumulate. And fast!

APRIL 17

Since the official newspapers don't print ads, all the streetlights, the telegraph and telephone posts are papered with advertisements. I bargained with my parents. I would write the ads and put them up if they would let me stop school. They accepted. Early this morning, I started in earnest:

FOR SALE, CHEAP AND QUICK, MAHOGANY BEDROOM SET, FLORENTINE STYLE DINING ROOM, PERSIAN RUGS, CHINA, PAINTINGS, FIXTURES, DISHES, SILVERWARE, MISCELLANEOUS.
BEST OFFER BUYS IT!

APRIL 21

My father ordered the wooden box which will contain our belongings. The Government had decided not only the weight, but also the content. Forbidden are jewelry, gold, fixtures, furniture, even picture frames.

APRIL 22

Today we went to the Israeli Embassy for our physicals, including vaccinations. Under the beautiful linden and mulberry trees in the garden, on the entrance steps, through the corridors, in and out the gate, the place swarmed with people. Standing in line to have our medical examination we saw mothers nursing babies, men praying *mincha*, *maariv* and *shacharit* (afternoon, evening, and morning prayers); women knitting shawls, sweaters, gloves, doing embroidery, changing babies, or playing cards and chess.

MAY 1

What an irony! Jews are now competing with each other to get rid of goods they had struggled a lifetime to acquire. In this competition my mother is a winner. Yesterday, a customer came to the house intending to buy a picture but left bending under the weight of a light fixture under one arm, and our cuckoo clock under the other.

Out of love, my mother decided against selling our August Forster piano, her childhood instrument which her parents had bought especially for her. Instead she plans to give it to one of our cousins before our departure.

MAY 10

Oh, my dear diary, a new problem is clouding our days. My darling Baba [paternal grandmother] has been watching our comings and goings with increasing anxiety. For the past six months, since Aunt Polly [her daughter] and family left for Israel, she has been living with us. In their rush to leave Romania, Aunt Polly and Uncle Chaym overlooked applying for a passport for Baba. "Old folks are the first ones to be allowed to emigrate," they said, trying to appease her and probably their conscience as well. "It will be only a matter of months before we'll be reunited."

Now her little world seems to fall apart. She has become apathetic. She shakes her head and murmurs incessantly, "My son is leaving me, my son is leaving me."

MAY 12

Baba has started a new habit, walking. Before, it was difficult to get her out of the house. Now she walks exhaustingly, leaving around noon and arriving at home after dark, completely drained. People told us they had seen her in the most incredible places, talking to strangers and telling them in Yiddish, the only language she knows, "My son is leaving me; my son is leaving me."

MAY 16

The wooden box arrived today. It is going to serve as my bed until we leave. Every night I climb on it with the help of a small stool.

Inside the box, my clever mother had installed hooks on which she hangs now the clothes we'll take with us to Israel. So, as of now, the box is serving two purposes, bed and chiffonier.

MAY 22

My mother spent the last three Sundays at Talcioc, the flea market, trying to sell what we weren't able to sell at home.

She packed our bric-a-brac into two big bundles and left the house at dawn in order to get a space on the market's ground, which she covered with a huge tablecloth. On top she piled clothes, unmatched dishes, my father's old galoshes, old books, and even picture frames. When she returned, she said, "Hell couldn't be worse than Talcioc. On one side, Romanian aristocracy exchanging jewelry or precious china for nothing, for a piece of bread, while on the other side pickpockets are selling their weekly take. Gypsies move around telling fortunes and stealing from the piles of those unfortunates screaming out their lungs to attract clients to their pathetic merchandise."

JUNE 1

I am so, so excited. Finally today we received our passports. My father ran out and bought a bottle of champagne to celebrate. Tomorrow, first thing in the morning we're going to the Israeli Embassy to obtain the date for our departure. It's real, it is happening!

JUNE 2, 4 A.M.

Oh, my God, this is the last thing we expected. Yesterday after we celebrated receiving our passport, Baba disappeared. We still hadn't found her at midnight. My father's terror knew no bounds. He ran out of the house. My mother and I couldn't sleep. Hours later, when it was almost dawn, the two of them came home. He found her sitting on a bench in a deserted farmer's market crying her heart out and singing, *Artzole, Shreib a brief tzu dein mama.* [Write a letter to your mother.]

JUNE 2, 7 P.M.

As if the trauma we had last night with Baba wasn't enough of a shock, this morning we got another one.

After we had waited again in the endless line at the Israeli embassy, the embassy secretary said that our date of departure is set for July 13, almost two weeks after our exit visas expire. "Don't worry," the secretary told my parents, observing how tense they had become, "This has happened to other people, too. All you have to do is to apply for an extension of your visa at the Department of Interior. I assure you it is only a formality."

JUNE 3

My parents didn't sleep all night. I heard them tossing and whispering. They decided that my mother would go to the Department of Interior to apply for an extension to our visa.

JUNE 6

My mother went to the Department of Interior to apply for an extension to our visa. She returned in good spirits. When she explained to the officer in charge the reason we need a visa extension, he said, "Leave your passports here, and come back a week from today."

JUNE 9

This is hard to believe! Today we received a postcard on which one word was printed in huge letters. NEGATIVE. What could it mean? Our hearts stopped beating. We turned the card over. The names and address were correct: ours.

Lately we had heard more and more about Jews receiving negative postcards. But our case was different. We had been approved already.

My mother refused to give up. "Don't panic," she said courageously. "Let's wait for my appointment. Only three more days."

JUNE 13, 7 P.M.

My father decided that we'd accompany my mother and wait for her at a coffee house close to the Department of Interior. My mother appeared after fifteen minutes. She looked at us with glassy eyes. "It was a mistake," she said in a bitter and tired voice, "a huge mistake." She laughed like a crazy woman.

She tried to imitate the officer's voice. "Didn't you receive a negative postcard?"

He didn't let her explain. "Listen, I'm sorry, but I've got my orders. Your passport as well as the passport of 800 other families was issued by mistake. They weren't signed by the right official. We are recalling all of them."

"What do we do now?" my mother cried. "We've sold everything. What's going to happen to us?"

"Look lady, I have no time for discussion. You've heard the answer. Leave or I'll call a policeman."

My mother ended her mockery in tears. We went home. For our family Yom Kippur 1950 arrived early, on June 13th.

EPILOGUE

Baba left for Israel in 1952. We kept applying for an exit visa every year. It took eight more years and seven more negative postcards before our saga came to an end, and our wish became reality. In December 1958 we reached the Promised Land. ♣

Four Generations of Women

Mildred Belle (1890-1978) **my grandmother**, wrote poems and diary pages when she'd finished her chores on the farm.

Doris Lucille (1920-1988) **my mother**, wrote poems, prose, journal jottings and stories when she'd finished cleaning the house or planting the garden.

I, Donna Lucille (born 1944) write poems, prose, and journal entries in between teaching college classes or after I take my sons or daughter to school.

Juliet Belle (born 1999) **my daughter**, runs in the back yard or the front yard, or in parks telling stories. Some of these she writes down. Some of these she tells to me. "Some I tell just to God," she says.

Each generation has promised the one before that she will preserve our writings.

Here they are, portions of a four generational memoir.

Donna Lucille Emerson

Mildred Emerson Dascomb
Last months with her mother, Eliza Emerson ("Tish")
1940

These are Mother's ravings toward the last. She talked incessantly. I wrote it down as she said it. Probably just to keep from going mad myself. She lived probably six or seven months after this. She knew something was terrible wrong – Poor Tish –

(She's taking off and putting on stockings, scraping them over her big toe.)

I don't want them like that. Now you see, that's all up. I want this down there – there. Now I'll have that down like that. Can I fix that other? I don't know where I should have it fixed, and she don't know where. I can't stand it. If I knew where it was I could fix it, but I don't know. I'm lost. I don't know what to do. Do you suppose I'm lost. I'm an awful lost child, Mildred, I'm lost. Can she stay on there? Well, I wish you'd see if that woman is all right. I don't know. I'm stuck. Oh, Mildred, how can you do that. Where can I go? I thought first I was discouraged and didn't know what to do. Now I'm stuck fast. Mildred, can you let me in there? She don't know where she is – that woman don't.

Mildred, I'm scared to death. Can I get by any of them? I don't know how to get by. She don't know about taking care of them. She says, "No!" She won't leave them here, but I don't know. But, if I could get by with those three children I'd be all right. Then she would let them pass along. She won't hold them there. See that one is on the line. She ought to sit up there. Can you sit her up there?

She feels bad, she doesn't want me to leave her. She's my child and I won't leave her. She can pass along there. Maybe she can out front. Maybe this woman don't want to keep her. She won't be up there will she, Mildred? She'll tell her she can't. I don't believe a word she says. Can't I get by you?

Oh yes, Mildred, I want her to come in here. She'll feel awful if I don't let her. Can't you, Mildred? I don't believe a word on there. And, Mildred, I can't stand it. She can't go in there. What'll I do for her? What's she going to do for me? I left her on the other side. ♣

Doris Lucille Dascomb Rhodes
As her son, Ralph, became a naval officer and went to Vietnam
JULY 1968

The morning dawned crying, sobbing – howling. Everything seemed wet, heavy soggy – it was a morning to sleep, lulled by the pattering rain drips – a sleep full of peaceful happy sleepy dreams. It was not a morning to say goodbye, to hold back the tears – not when the whole world was weeping.

Twenty-two years ago there was no specter of war to threaten the tiny baby boy, not 20, 18, 16 years ago was the danger so personally imminent. But this day was here. The dreadful, fearful day had arrived and what could one do to change the irrevocable course of events down to this day. There was no choice; the series of events had come to this. What choice did one have; was there something one could have done to thwart this? Did we do everything we could? No – it wouldn't have been right, it would have been all wrong – wrong to pull strings, use friends, plead or beg – but was it right to go along with a system that you disagree with so completely, not to do these things to protect a life so dear, sweet and wonderful? Born in war, raised in war, off to war – war, war, war, was there no peace, no contentment, no happy carefree living left?

I'll fix lunch – back to the primitive duty of motherhood – feed them, coddle and cuddle them, keep them warm and comfortable – the mother need, the outward symbol of inner love – feed him.

So tall, so fair, so handsome, so manly – is there a purer love than parental love? The lump that had been in my throat for months loomed large and painful. I prayed to have the strength not to cry, not to blubber, not to clutch and drag at him – the strength to let him go as a man unafraid and worthy of a dignified farewell. God, go with him – do not worry, my darling, I have sent God with you – and now the tears can come and dissolve the painful lump a little, just a little for it will take a lifetime of tears to calm the fear for the safety of a son going off to war. ♣

Doris Lucille Dascomb Rhodes
On the death of her mother, Mildred
JUNE-JULY 1978

Mom (Mildred): "You can do anything you want to me for I have the guts." (sitting up in bed)

Doris: "Do you mean courage, Mom?"

Mom: "Yes, courage. It's leaving me. Hit me over the head with guts. Something just left me. I'm losing them. Let me out of here. I've got to get guts. But they are there – right there."

JULY 1, 1978

Mom died. Just leaned back on my arm, sighed and was gone. I didn't know what was happening; and yet deep down I knew but hoped she had just fainted. One doesn't mistake that. I told Ann Cummings (her roommate) to call a nurse quick. There was no pulse when she came. She looked so peaceful, it seemed as if all the lines left her face –

I had been late getting to the hospital that a.m. Everyone called to ask about Mom. When I walked into Mom's room, her curtain was drawn, Mom was sitting up in the middle of the bed stark naked saying as I came near, "No one here to take care of me." I hugged her skinny shoulders and eased the hospital gown around her. She felt so warm and kept saying, "Skin me alive." I started rubbing her back with lotion. Combed her hair and put it up and resumed rubbing her back. This felt so good to her. She calmed down but still kept saying, "Skin me alive." And then just left me. It seemed as if she had just waited for me and yet I shall never be sure that she knew I was there. I hope she knew that and how very much we all loved her. ♣

Donna Emerson
Age 29, San Francisco
FEBRUARY 7, 1973

In the pouring rain on a lonely but calm Monday night I took myself to the movies. Fellini's *Roma*. There I saw far more than a film.

As I sat waiting (for the movie to begin) in the lobby I was attracted to a petite woman with a lovely face, white, white hair and wearing a bonnet. Tied under her chin like a little girl's.

I felt I knew her or had known her, or would know her. She appeared happy, well attended by two young men, who looked to me like art students. From the art school two streets down from my apartment, on Russian Hill. I wondered if she were the mother or grandmother of one, but no, she didn't seem to be behaving as a mother. Most of all she seemed alive and vital. So much that I didn't think about her age at all. More lively, perceptive, and exuberant, perhaps, than all the older people I've known.

She leaned over to the one next to me – we were on benches that sat at right angles to each other.

She said, "That's a nice coat," referring to mine. My U.S. Marine's jacket, purchased at the surplus store. She and I looked at each other. I wore my pink crocheted cap off the side of my head and we smiled, both in our hats. The boy mentioned liking her show at the Art Museum, especially the 1915 photographs of Yosemite.

She twinkled, "Yes, that's when I was chasing my husband of the time around that mountain."

A big expressive smile.

She wore large glasses whose frames were clear pink. All of a sudden I knew that she was Imogen Cunningham. The photographer whose work I had at home. The ones whose crumpled sheets were what I tried to make happen in my bed prints. She knew the zone system without ever studying with Ansel Adams. White whites and black blacks and all in-between. She was probably with him in Yosemite in 1915!

There we all were, beaming at each other. One of the young men leaned over, whispered to me, "She'll be 90 next month."

She laughed when I did at the film. She spoke in an animated way to her escorts during it. When it was over, I turned around and her eyes met mine. We both smiled at each other.

3-15-73

I ran into Imogen again today. We've seen each other several times. We do our laundry at the same laundromat. I stood last week and just looked at her pulling her laundry cart up the hill. She gave me a lecture today in the intersection at Hyde Street about my camera. As she gazed at it slung over my shoulder, she said, "35 mm is fine for news of the world, but you should get yourself a real camera!"

Juliet Emerson
Age 4, written down by her mother, Donna Emerson
JULIET'S MORNING STORY GAME
NOVEMBER 26, 2003

Pretend we're horses. *(We trot and whinny.)*
You'll be the mother and I'll be the baby.
We live in this stall in the living room.
And pretend my Daddy is gone, away, maybe dead.

And you might marry a mean man
Who hurts us.

There he is, the mean one,
And he's hurt us and we cry.
We lie down near each other on the meadow
(We huddle on the floor, holding each other.)
And are hurt *(We both whimper.)*
But I get better and you don't.

(Juliet gets up on her feet and frolics.
Juliet then picks up a yellow pillow and hands it to me saying)
Here's some hay. It will make you feel better.
(I eat the hay and Juliet looks satisfied.)

Then we find our Daddy here, our good Daddy.
He's under this rock and he's alive!
Oh now we have our Daddy back again! *(We prance and dance.)* ♣

1970

Diary of a Teenager

In 1970 I was a 15-year-old high school sophomore in a suburban Washington D.C. public school. That spring, my English teacher, Mr. Roy Simmons, gave us the assignment of writing journals; it was an assignment that changed my life and set me on the path to being a writer. I continue to write in my journal with a fountain pen on lined notebook paper kept in a clasp folder – the same way I began in that 10th grade English class.

Liz Rhodebeck

Tuesday, February 24, 1970

Rehersal went bad today—at least for me. I just felt so blah and useless. The people are so meaningless to me and yet I stick with it. When I got home I couldn't wait to get out of the pants—I don't know why. They just felt so dirty, wrong. I don't feel lively after rehersals like I used to. The pants are a symbol of the "Tribe"—something I'm not really part of, never will be and don't want to be. Yet here I am. I can't stand the record "Hair" anymore—and I used to like it. When I came home though I am so full of psychedelic trash I can't stand it and reject and counteract it in everyway possible.

How about a nice hot cup of tea, some quiet music like Simon and Garfunkle (or Burt Baby) something soft and silky (like a robe), and someone decent to chat with (or a good book)?

And yet I don't want to drop it. It's something I want to do, work at and I usually enjoy until the end (and it drags) *what?* or I know I could be doing something more worthwhile. I'm not satisfied. I'm hungry for something useful to do – productive, fulfilling, helpful, giving.

Will I never get to work on the D.C. Program?

Have I ceased to live and now mearly exist? I know not! Maybe Ras' board will give me something to do.

Shall I skip rehersal Thursday for the D.C. Program?

LET ME GO!

Wednesday, February 25, 1970

We had a "cut-down" session in English today, but I'm not too sure what it accomplished. Mr. Simmons said he let us do it because it gave the class some kind of unity, and he hoped to reduce the "dislike" for him by letting them speak freely, to show he wanted to give them a chance. But I don't think anyone had any worthwhile comments, not even Mr. Simmons. I have trouble understanding that class!

I read "The Lost Phoebe" by Theodore Dreiser. For some reason it touched me very deeply; it made me cry. I felt sorry for Henry Reifsneider and yet very happy for him. I was happy that even after 48 years of marriage, he and Phoebe were still so devoted and lovable to each other. I was sorry that he was going to have to live all alone after she died. Had the children been living at home, I don't think it would have been so bad, but she was the only world he knew, and a joyous one at that. I have often wondered if old people must get tired of each other after so many years or if love dies out for it is sometimes hard to see uniowship between parents now a days. But reading this just made me feel hopeful, perhaps because when you're young you don't want to grow old; but once you are old, perhaps you don't mind it after all. I think I felt some pity toward the end when he was searching, but I don't think it was just that. Here again I was amazed at his love for his wife yet was frustrated at his persistance. I think the passage that touched me most was the part where he recalles their youth, her "girlish figure" the spring of love. I know I can believe love is the strongest and most endurable and lasting thing in the world.

Friday, February 27, 1970

"When you think you know someone very well, do you know them very well?"

I think the most exciting thing about living is other people. Even in one individual there is so much you can learn about him. And to complicate it even more, people are always changing. You can never know a person to the fullest for each day can bring a new experience and situation that you have never had the chance to react to, therefore, something else you don't know. I have a friend I thought I had evaluated pretty well when zap! I find we have something new in common. And then I find she is doing something, I thought she would never be interested in. Now I want to get to know more of her—I think she would be interesting. I think change is ~~the~~ one of the most stimulating things in life.

"When you're through changing, you're through." So true! You must seek change within yourself for everybody could be better. Sometimes just acting different, like running around, stretching if you're quite reserved or conformed, or sitting quietly and doing nothing if you're generally busy, will refreshen you greatly.

pril 5 —   Weather —
                  Partly cloudy
                  Breezy
Plans   Temp 50°
        None —
        Relax and enjoy day!

Happenings!
Awake refreshed!
Had 2 cups o' coffee!
Back to bed to read paper!
Phyllis called! my day off to good start!
Watched T.U. News — 8:30
Have had breakfast — egg —
Taken my Decadron pill — 1 grapefruit
It is now — 9:15 — Will get washed!
Will get dressed in smock —
Will tidy bedroom — make bed —   dust
Out to finish kitchen — all done!
10:15 Dressed + ready for days activities.
Went down to fix door — got mail — bill!
Rachel called!
Put Poissetta in Sun!
It is already 1:15 and I am
having lunch! Spanish Rice — Beets
Will rest a bit later! Pumpkin Pie
+ tea — later
I called Willma! Talked a long —
time! Mostly me! Willma gave
me an answer that I shall try

ta remember."
Tis 3:30   Kendy called!
Nice chat!
Took my Bursites pill!
Just heard man throw my
paper on porch! Will go
down + get it soon! Way out!!
Am going to lie down — not to
sleep — just to rest!
Sky is getting gray + gloomy! not
Let's hope my "Bursites" does
flare up! Talked with Betty T
(my partner at #234)! Went down to
get my paper — picked up a post
card from Hawai. Took my "pill" at
3:30 P.m — next one due — 7:30
                              didn't
Tis 7.P.m! I'm about to get into
my pink nightie and gown! Had
supper — chicken noodle soap   hot
          Pears — will have chocolate late
Rose B. called! Tell Willma she will
not call tomorrow night. going to a nephew
May will get in touch later

1973

Mimi's Writing Tablet

My grandmother, Catherine Burke, never kept a diary or journal, as far as I know, until the last year of her life. It was a difficult year – she had cancer, her memory was failing, she lived alone, she didn't drive. She kept a daily record on a simple white tablet of what she did each day, or what she was planning to do, and whether the sun was out. When my cousin Katy gave me her journals a few years ago, I was thrilled. Being a journal keeper myself, I expected to find passages that would allow me insight into the woman I loved so much. Instead I found these lists, spare and repetitive, but nonetheless lively. As I copy them, and type her exclamation marks at the end of every phrase or word, her abbreviated o' for "of", I feel her particular style, her pauses, reminiscent of Emily Dickinson, and her unflagging spirit. (I also notice how often I called her, several times a week, which makes me enormously happy to know.) I am grateful to her for simply writing, for picking up the pen and using it as a companion, a guide, a means of expression that connects her to me again.

Kendra Kopelke

TUESDAY – JAN. 30 – 73

Had a good night's rest!
Waked at 7:45! 2 cups o' coffee
out + only 10 a.m.! Phone rang! Paul
was at Pop's. Would stop over! He
had driven his mother to Annapo-
lis ~ I fixed him – or – I shud say
he fixed "him" a toasted egg
sandwich – juice – coffee! I
joined with a ½ cup o' coffee! We
had such a nice chat! He's great!
Talked with Kendy! Home with a
sore throat! Tis 3 pm + no one has
called ~ no mail either ~ The
sun is shining! which means arm
is ok! I have on a new smock ~
so feel fresh + clean.

7:30 Tired – will get ready for bed!
but stay up – by phone till 8 pm!
Mrs. Brenner from 234 – exparent
friend o Yvette's called! Wanted to
visit me tonight!!

THURSDAY – FEB 1 – 9:30 A.M.

Had my coffee – House all
tidy – except kitchen – not
hungry – so can't decide on
breakfast – guess I'll make
it a brunch! . . . 10:40 a.m.
Had scrambled eggs! ～ apples!
Good ～ dishes done ～ kitchen
ok～ all set for an exciting
day! Started fine ～ got mail
a nice "Cheery Hello card"
from Mildred (Richard's wife)! plus
read paper – do puzzle – not tired-
Talked with Willma + Rose!
Meals were good. Well balanced! I am washed –
pink gown + robe! Feel clean + good.
Hope to remember to see Flip at 8 p.m. –
Flip's program was not on – instead "S.S."
Turned on radio – but did
not listen long! Till tomorrow.

SATURDAY FEB 3, 1973!

Feel fine! <u>rested</u> + <u>relaxed</u>!
Plans for today! –

Make <u>no</u> tel. calls – but
hope for some!
No <u>T.V.</u> till 5 p.m. (Welk Show)
8 p.m. Archie
8:30 Bridget
9:00 Mary Tyler Moore

Wash out panties –
Hope for some mail!
<u>Maybe</u> write to Margaret & Mildred
Remember to tell Phyllis about Rhododendron – (beautiful)
but do not talk ov Rachel –
who is in <u>great</u> pain with
broken foot – feels <u>alone</u> +
(sometimes, <u>not</u> <u>often</u>) – feels <u>low</u> –
when foot still achy after <u>7</u> <u>or</u> <u>8</u> <u>weeks</u>!
Try to carry out some o' Monday plans!
1)wrote to Margaret

Willma called! Had a <u>good</u> chat!
Thinks I should <u>relax</u>! + <u>take</u> care
o' me! I shall start <u>pronto</u>! Turning in
at 8 p.m. Watch T.V. from bed.

DEC 10 – SUNDAY!

New resolutions!
No more <u>chat</u> calls till <u>after</u> holidays.
No more feeling sorry for myself
No more <u>worrying</u> about "how to get to Dr."
<u>Try</u> to be the old me! C'est sera-sera." ♣

Friday + Saturday

Weather 6th - 7th
Getting Clear - Cold
cloudy Sunny

Things I need!
2 refills for
fountain pens –
Red + black pen
Potatoes

✓ Remind Willma
about Rose
Water Plants –
✓ Put Poinsetta in
Sun!
✓ ✓ Take Decadron pill (one)
✓ Take Bursites pills
every 4 hrs - 1:30
5:30
✓ Watch "Dial for $
Chan II - 9:30 # 2 # 7:30
7:30 8:00 6:30 7:00 8
Archie etc 9:00

✓ Eggs
✓ Milk { Evap
Han di whips ✓
Ammaia –
Les Toil
Ajax –

Things that happened

Willma called! Friday
Rose called!
Lawyer called about tax
Helen tossed up paper
Long chat with Helen
Sat.?
Mrs H. visited (social.?)
Johnson Bros. came!
love my cola T.V –
Willma called
Mary A. came over
to visit! Rose Miller called!

Things I've done

Had good breakfast! –
Tidied Kitchen –
Tidied bedroom –
Called Rose B! (mustn't)
let Rose call me when not busy
learned how to work
colored TV. Johnson men
Showed me how!

To bed
early Mary

1974

Pearly Yuni's Journal

My mother, Pearly Yuni, was a housewife and mother who hadn't written creatively until she was diagnosed with cancer at age 59. She refused surgery, treated the cancer holistically and joined a support group. The group leader gave writing assignments that encouraged self expression and my mother began her journals. My sister and I found them after she died. She was like a tree that was cut down early and then blossomed.

She wrote in spiral school notebooks, stenographer's pads, on loose papers and the backs of used envelopes. "I am in a frenzy to get to the A&P, to get to the bank. I must pay my bills," she wrote. "How dare I write when I am on a treadmill of undone chores. Writing is Nero fiddling, my inner turmoil – Rome burning."

The physical pain and the journaling made her less narcissistic and more humane. It was this new and truer self I wanted to know. All I wanted of my mother's belongings were the journals. She and I had had a bad relationship.

I was looking for answers. What I read hurt me but I also felt gratified and proud of her talent. I found in her journal stories the mother I hadn't had in life.

Wendy Hoffman

Pearly Yuni
THE SILVER BRUSH

I loved Mr. Sokalov. I was two – I remember sitting with him in the park. He was a returned soldier in the First World War mending his wounds – I found this out later. He loved me. He thought I was the smartest and prettiest little girl in the world and said so. He always had time for me. My father, handsome, quick, never did. Mr. Sokalov took me to the park sometimes with my mother. He smiled at my mother. I remember his arms, the calmness, I felt safe. (Until I married him, I felt safe in Steve's arms). I remember sun and grass and bliss in the park. I sang songs.

In those days, people took in boarders. To get this lovely apartment, my parents took in Mr. Sokalov to help pay the rent. My earliest memory, Mr. Sokalov carried me all over the apartment. We were in his room. His silver comb and brush glittered. They were on his chest of drawers. I picked up the brush. He let me play with it all day. I left it in my parents' room. Mama, 19, Daddy, 23. My father, jealous, volatile, found it there. Storms unleashed. My mother's denials. The reproach and anger in her eyes at me. I did not know why. I knew I did something wrong. I did not know what.

I pieced that together as a grown woman. I have been looking for Mr. Sokalov all my life, but on the way, I married my father. I never sing songs. They never pass my lips.

Pearly Yuni
WATER

I was young and just had learned to swim. We were at the beach and it was difficult to learn with the high waves.

Momma and I and my sister were alone all week and on weekends Daddy came. That was a joy. Momma treated him like a nice guest.

It was so peaceful. Daddy came on Friday late in the day. Now I could not wait for tomorrow. Please, Daddy, come with me, please. I have something to show you. Daddy looked so handsome in his white suit and striped shirt and straw hat. Daddy hated the sand. He stepped on the beach gingerly in his white city shoes.

I plunged into the water. I swam away. It was my proud moment. I was doing well. I looked up to catch Daddy's eyes and to see his pride. Daddy was looking far into the horizon thinking of business. Daddy always thought of business. Business, he always said, came first. He was looking at the big ships so far away they looked like little sail boats, like the toys in my baby sister's bathtub. I looked up. I could not believe he wasn't watching. Daddy, look at me. Look at me. The roar of the waves drowned out my voice. Daddy's gone now but I still feel the cry in my throat. Look at me, Daddy. Look at me. ❧

1984

In Guatemala

At age 38, I was out of shape and restless with wanderlust, so I quit my job, gave up my Corona del Mar apartment and set out alone on an 11-month bus, boat and train journey to South America's tip. When I left California in mid-1984, I possessed only the vaguest itinerary, knew but a handful of Spanish words, and carried a pack on my back. On other treks around the world, I met backpackers who were bereft because their travel journals had been lost or stolen. I wasn't willing to take that risk, so I wrote diary entries inside aerograms, on the backs of postcards and on ragged pages torn from notepads, and mailed them to a sister. I knew that I was traveling roads along which backpackers had been known to "disappear," so I also recognized that my notes would chart my course if I was held captive or killed.

Orman Day

who had done a little television acting. He had had a little tough luck on his trip. For one, he caught hepatitis. For another, he was attacked and chased around a restaurant by two guys in Mexico. His most fascinating story, tho', was about a bus ride he had in El Salvador. He boarded with a swiss girl, but for some reason, she took a seat at the back and he, at the front. During the ride, an Salvadorean man started leaning against the girl, so she called for Robert to sit between her and him. The guy started leaning against Robert. Then he pulled out a hand grenade. Robert at first was shocked, needless to say. The man pretended to pull the pin of the grenade and then went "Ka-pow," flinging out his hands. Robert was horrified, but he figured he better humor the guy

AUGUST, ANTIGUA, GUATEMALA

In Antigua, I met a blond, slightly built San Franciscan named Robert who had done a little television acting. He had had a little tough luck on his trip. For one, he caught hepatitis. For another, he was attacked and chased around a restaurant by two guys in Mexico. His most fascinating story, tho, was about a bus ride he had in El Salvador. He boarded with a Swiss girl, but for some reason, she took a seat at the back and he, at the front. During the ride, a Salvadorian man started leaning against the girl, so she called for Robert to sit between her and him. The guy started leaning against Robert. Then he pulled out a hand grenade. Robert at first was shocked, needless to say. The man pretended to pull the pin of the grenade and then went "Ka-pow," flinging out his hands. Robert was horrified, but he figured he better humor the guy, so he laughed and started gesturing with his hands too. He told his companion to go along too. Robert was particularly disturbed, tho, when the man pretended to explode the grenade near some children on the bus. Robert told the girl that if the man pulled the pin, she was to break open a window and throw it outside. He figured they would have eight seconds. Finally, Robert told the man in broken Spanish that he must think he's a big man because he had the grenade. The man eventually put away the grenade, put his head against Robert's shoulder, and dissolved into tears. Robert stroked his head. Within a stop or two, the man got off the bus.

That night I decided it was time to get up on the edge – by going to El Salvador – despite warnings about Westerners who had disappeared.

OCTOBER, PERU

An American woman in another country told me that sometimes her friends write to say they're broke. She buys them a birthday card. Between it she puts another sheet with small holes in it. In the holes, she puts cocaine. A postal inspector doesn't feel the cocaine and doesn't open the envelope because it's only a relatively thin card.

On the other hand, I suspect that the thick envelopes of postcards I send from such drug smuggling locales as Columbia, Peru and Bolivia are opened. They, of course, contain a mind altering substance of a quite different kind: the written word. ♣

1988

Nebraska Tracks Journal & Glory Down My Road

I give my journals titles, just like books. My "Nebraska Tracks Journal" came from the joyful experiences I gained as I traveled by auto the Main Street of America, the pounded road of pioneers. "Glory Down My Road" is a journal that holds my impressions, thoughts and feelings on my journeys in the Adirondacks, in Indiana, and Nebraska. The beauty around us is such a tremendous gift, an uplifting catalyst, I feel it's important for the writer/artist to teach about the beauty on this Earth.

Kathleen Marie Leary

from **MY NEBRASKA TRACKS JOURNAL**

MAY 1988

I travel by auto the Main Street of America, the pounded road of pioneers. My journey East to West is straight across the lower part of the state.

The Nebraska rain taps my skin on a dusty day. In Dawson County, I study a train as it rolls across the vast fields. Trains and weather vanes ask to be counted in Nebraska. When I visit the grasslands and wetlands, I view geese with their unsteady winged rhythms over the Platte River. And far west, I am a pioneer – in mind – as I step onto prairie, and onto the corners of flatland, negotiate the rugged rock bluffs which rise high above our world. Such striking landmarks shift, depending on from where they are seen, so nobody necessarily views the same rock as the same. But everyone here must know the mystical feeling of Nebraska perceptions, and on clear nights, all must touch a star.

MAY 6
GRAND ISLAND

The harsh wind picks up pebbles which dart my extremities and burn the skin. This is tornado season. The dirt of the fields blows in low streamlined clouds across the road. The sound of the wind is like that of a thousand sheets frocked and flocked together on a clothes line, all blowing against each other.

MAY 10 (MILD WIND)

I love the light of a distant train engine as it comes into my direction. My feelings are comfortable yet a bit tossed as we each meet in the present and say goodbye as it passes by. In the desolate country, the train enters like a friend. Afterwards, when the train is gone, I place my eyes upon the Platte River. I know it will stay with me, be my guide for a long while.

from **GLORY DOWN MY ROAD**

MAY 4, 1990

Flowers in fields along the roadway bloom in pastel blues and violets. I don't know the names of flowers. I'm not an erudite naturalist. Just a lover of pretty things.

I suppose every talent I possess, and every charm that I perhaps manage, is wild. I'm an untrained artist. My sister calls me untamed. I don't know how art is taught in art schools, but I want to study painting sometime. . . . I like to look at picture books of the lady who raised gorillas in the jungle, and the woman who climbed up the Himalayas. With these women I identify. I dream to trek across India, but I will be fine if I don't. My present love is in breathing the Adirondacks. I'm learning that how I spend my solitary life is my religion, and I'm finding that art is spiritual. Seeing outside of me and touching it through my eyes and keeping it with my pen is my way of knowing people and the world.

SEPTEMBER 9
SKY ABOVE AN INDIANA FARM

It's the weekend in South Bend. Hot and humid, stale in the city. We could use some wind. I drive on.

There's a pink house north of the city. And a quarter horse farm reminds me of the outside of South Bend, tells me of the pretty things that neighbor on my mind. I drive more.

The sky seems to be a reflection of me. Everchanging. Feeling pretty as sun, and sometimes, wearing grey.

I see the first birds of Autumn to congregate in swift, and dart south, streamlining the blue above. . . . The afternoon sun drops upon Mayflower Road. Shines in vertical ribbons that crack the afternoon hour. That sun wipes translucent haze across the cornfields growing tall, and touches the top of the silo. A jet plane is like a dream across the sky. One, and then another catch my eyes. My car moves on.

SEPTEMBER 13
ABOUT NEBRASKA

I'm tired. Are you? Footloose are we, with just an uncluttered sky, streamed by birds of summer. Let's drag our feet and then, when we are truly awake again, we shall run across the prairie. Let us be at leisure, and in fun wrap up this end of day. Challenge the quiet, ride the dry wind, and recite the myths of an old, spacious America. Let us follow the old trails of unconvention for our day and speak in open spaces, and leave our own trails of song.

1990

The Professor

Approaching the end of my ninth decade, I still enjoy writing and reading, the latter courtesy of the Andrew Heiskell Library of Talking Books for the visually impaired. Sharing memories and daily experiences with the man who has been my husband for 69 years is also a joy, as is my daughter's TLC and the real and email visits from my son and grandson who live in Japan. From the cornucopia of attractions that awaited me after I retired from the faculty of Kingsborough Community College, one of my choices was to assume the role of a student again. As can be seen from this journal entry, unexpected obstacles arose.

Terry Miller

THE PROFESSOR

The professor is tall and thin, awkward, uncomfortable about beginning a class, meeting all these strangers for the first time. He'd much prefer to remain in the solitude of the winter vacation. His attitude plus an instinctive expectation that a teacher be older than I, forgetting totally that that is not possible anymore, causes me a jolt of surprise when he begins talking about having been caught up in the activism of the 60s. It is a shock to realize that my essay teacher is the age of my children.

I watch the professor, dressed the way academics like to dress, in sloppy wide wale corduroy pants, either gray or tan, ingratiate himself with the students who are film majors. But I overlook his attempt to be younger than his age because he knows the essay, from Virginia Woolf's about the death of the moth to Lewis Thomas's about death in general. One day I go to his office for feedback on my essay.

From the beginning there has been something peculiar about my reactions in this class, something I don't understand. I am a confident 70-year-old woman with a lot to feel satisfied about, someone who, in youth, was insouciant, bold, disrespectful of authority. Why have I suddenly turned into a timid school girl? I tiptoe into his office. No, I actually wait at the threshold of a room where he is typing, and when he looks up, ask, "Am I, as a mere auditor of the course, entitled to make demands on your time?"

I think I've figured it out. We're both a little scared of each other. He's aware that I'm older, with more of the coin of the realm than he has. . . . the doctorate . . . and in psychology yet. He is afraid that I will *know* him. And I am afraid that my writing will turn out to be laughable, not humorous, laughable, and that he will *know* me.

He sends me to his office while he finishes what he is typing. When he comes in he takes a seat behind the desk and opens the interview . . . with my line, "How can I help you?" I tell him of my dissatisfaction with the way the essay is developing, the ending, the order of things. "You mean you want some help with the structure?" The schoolgirl nods. I give him the 13-page manuscript. He asks if that is my only copy and I tell him that some of the pages have not been duplicated. He scolds about that and goes off to xerox the whole thing for me. While he's gone, the phone begins to ring. And ring. And ring. What is protocol when you're in someone's office and the person whose office it is is doing a favor for you and his phone rings? I sit and listen to the ring. When he returns I tell him the phone rang like crazy and he asks why I didn't answer it.

The interview is not yet over. Something causes me to bring a hand to the open neck of my shirt. An odd piece of wire is there. What is it? This is not the time or place to investigate further. In no time I realize that this is the wire from my underwire bra that has come loose. I can't force it back. Does it show? I hope he only knows flat chested women so that he'll have no idea of the identity of this metal at my neck. What to do. It won't go back. Perhaps I can whisk it out and use it to make some grand gesture? Poise would be being able to remove it and walk to the end of the room where the waste basket is. The timid person lacks poise. I do with this what I had done with the telephone. Nothing. ♣

1991

SCUD War: Israel

I have kept a diary since I came to Israel from America. Unfortunately, everyday life in Israel is very often connected to great drama and cataclysmic events. When my four children were growing up, my husband travelled extensively. Living here was not easy for a newcomer, but through it all I always kept a diary. My daughter asks me how I did it. I really don't know. I just wrote in the midst of it all.

The first Gulf War began on January 16, 1991, and ended February 28, 1991. For Israelis, this was a very unusual war. Because of Saddam Hussein's threats to send chemical and biological warheads into Israel if attacked by America, gas masks were distributed to everyone in the country as well as syringes for self-application of atropine against toxic poisoning. Though Israel had no direct involvement with this war, Iraq sent 39 SCUD missiles into the country day and night. Each time the sirens blew, all of Israel rushed to sit in their 'safe rooms' where windows were sealed with plastic and duct tape and floor rags were stuffed under the doors to keep out poisonous fumes. Everyone put on gas masks, turned on TV and radio and waited for instructions.

Ruth Beker

To sit here and think. Is this the end? Is this my last day? Is this what I am supposed to be doing if it is? Will it be now, later tonight, tomorrow? Will it be one or three or five?

SCUDS is what I am talking about. Will it be chemical? Biological? God forbid atomic? If not now, when?

Saddam has so many friends, like the French, that grand old civilization dying to apologize for him, help him out. "If you've got the money honey I've got the time." "Moolah" that's the magic word.

Who can sleep. My friend says she has no more patience. For anything. She says everything she does takes at least five times as long and she doesn't feel like doing it anyway. Everyone is home before dark and stays there. Though some here-and-there people are starting to visit in the neighborhood, but not without gas masks and: *Come back soon. Don't forget your mask. Call when you get there. Maybe stay home?*

Nobody wants to stay home alone. So many even long-divorced men have moved back to stay with ex-wives and their children to keep them company leaving weeping inconsolable sweethearts behind.

Eli, a friend, sleeps at the old age home now to keep his mother company. Old age? Sounds like a curse doesn't it. It sure is now for anyone who is old, not strong and has to go into a sealed room, put on a gas mask and wait with beating tired heart for the all clear. He's always been close to his mother. It also has something to do with her suffering in the Holocaust.

The kids still aren't running outside. No one likes the idea of thinking that if there is a siren their child is not at home. Sometimes the kids can't stay home another minute so they go to a friend, the siren rings and they want you to pick them up.

But there's a good chance that on the way you'll hear the siren. You are supposed to pull the car over, close the windows, doors, vents. Put on your gas mask. Turn on the radio. And wait, hoping the scud is conventional, doesn't land on your head and is far away from you and everyone. And if God forbid it is close, that a Patriot will get it, all the parts crashing down but not over your beautiful head or burning your car to look like all the cars do on television after a scud has hit.

It's suspended living. No one makes plans. I don't know how the soldiers feel in the desert. I imagine a little like us. It is the waiting we have in common. If there is no siren, then you expect it. If it just happened, you think more must be coming.

I go to bed with: my walkman, TV controls, telephone, flashlight, gas mask hanging on the door knob, lights everywhere. Television on day and night. To warn you that a scud is on its way and hurry to your safe room. The TV tells you where it is supposed to land and who has to immediately put on gas masks. Friends call to make sure you hear the sirens and are in your safe room. As if we can sleep, not me anyway. Everyone here has taken in relatives, especially older people and those who can't take the tension in the area where most of the strikes are directed. My girlfriend calls to tell me she can't stand it anymore. There are two grandmothers and they both drive her crazy. They are nervous and think this is the end. And her two married sisters with their children.

A friend came by for a minute in the morning. She said she wasn't afraid, well, not so much in the daylight. She showed me a newspaper clipping of her gorgeous son, a paratrooper. So beautiful, so young, covering his face, crying because he lost his buddy, his best friend in a border killing.

All of Israel, from north to south, east to west, is waiting and praying that America and the allied forces will win over Saddam very soon and we can rip off the scotch tape and the plastic in the sealed room, spill out the bottled water, put the canned goods in the kitchen, dump the gas masks way back in the closet along with the atropine injection in case of. . . .

You watch on television the armies going to and fro, you watch the generals, the heads of state, you watch everything. Television, its picture, its sound is between me and the night and the war.

I'm always threatening not to read the newspaper anymore. But of course I will and so will we all. We can't help it. Our future is written there. Instead of counting sheep we count Patriots, Apaches, Cobras.

My aching heart. ♣

1992

The Paper Father

Back in 1992, being in the middle of the journey of my life and having no one to talk to, I began a journal in which I established a dialogue with my deceased father. He had passed on almost 30 years earlier from stomach cancer when he was only 36 and I was only 15. I never knew him that well because he worked all the time and I was a kid and didn't know any better. Anyway, I thought if I could talk to him today he would understand and perhaps even help me comprehend and muddle through the tough issues in my life.

Michael Estabrook

JULY 4

Well Dad, I'm 44 years old today,
good a day as any day
to begin writing to you –
talking to you –
so much to catch up on,
so much to tell you.
You've been gone now 29 years,
29 years, Twenty-Nine Years!
God. But enough of that. I know.
I know, if He didn't
want you, didn't have a Purpose
for you He wouldn't have
taken you so young.
Yes, I know all about it.
But enough,
enough for now.

JULY 5

I'm stuck, Dad, in the middle
of this mid-life crisis, and
it doesn't seem to be
abating. In fact, it's worsening,
and that's, I think,
the primary reason for my

talking to you.
You see, Dad, a man
only has his father.

– But what do you mean? –

I mean moms are there and
friends are fun
and wives are around and
all the support people like bosses,
neighbors, doctors, preachers, lawyers . . .
are helpful, but
no one knows, truly knows,
a man like his own father does.
The others don't even come close.
Who can know what I feel
better than you? Who?

– I don't think anyone can. –

Right.
For example, Patti has to go
back to work after all these years,
after 18 years of being
a stay-at-home mom
because David starts college in two
months and I don't make
enough money on my own to send him.

– Oh, really? Can't you work two jobs? –

No, it still wouldn't be enough.
Just imagine that. I have
three college degrees, 20 years work
experience and I can't even scrape up
enough god-damned money
to send my kid to college
without help, without taking out loans,
without my poor wife having
to go back to work.
It's disgusting, I'm a failure.

– No, well now, wait a minute. –

No Dad, hold on, I'm not finished.
Our daughter, Laura, she's 15
and she's eating us alive. God what spunk
that kid has. I know you'd
be crazy about her, but
I'm glad about it,
about all her spunk I mean, because
she needs to be tough today.
Women have come a long
way in 30 years, they're independent,
educated, confident, self-possessed.
They don't need men much anymore

for money or for sex,
for that matter, or for anything.

– No? –

There's no more putting a female
up on a pedestal, Dad,
where she belongs.

– No? –

Consequently, many men feel smaller,
threatened, unnecessary, and
they're lashing out abusing women,
striking them, stabbing them, shooting them,
raping them, killing them . . .

– What! –

Yes, Dad, they're cowards, dirty,
spineless cowards.

– How can men hurt women? What's wrong
with them? Why don't we lock them up? –

We try,
but probably there are too many.
It's a whole movement of dirty,
sniveling, small-minded cowards.

– It's disgusting! –

Bastards!

– Louts! –

Ball-less bastards!

– Aren't men men anymore? –

No.

JULY 6

I knew, Dad, that you'd
understand how
I'm feeling.
I've failed as a breadwinner,
and as a father too.
Let me back up a moment;
see what you'd say,
about Laura.
One week ago we sent her
to Europe, to Belgium
for three weeks, an exchange
program of sorts.

– All the way to Europe? –

Yes. But she's homesick,
miserable, absolutely miserable
and bored and . . .

– So what's the problem? Let
her come home early –

Really?

– Why of course, she doesn't
belong in Europe,
does she? Jesus –

Yes, I see.
You're right. I see.

JULY 7

– Back to your wife having to go
to work. –

Yes?

– Is there no other way? –

We could move. It's very expensive
to live here in Massachusetts.

– Where? –
(He looks at me stunned.)

Massachusetts.

– How in the hell did you
get in Massachusetts? Whatever happened
to Staten Island, and to Central New Jersey? –

I got a job promotion,
and I wanted to get my family away
from New Jersey and all the
industrial pollution: the streams are
ruined, the land is ruined,
the air is ruined.
You should see Elizabeth where you
were born, my God, it's almost uninhabitable.
The whole place has become known
as Cancer Alley.

(There's a long silence.)

– I guess I can relate to that.
It's good that you moved, son.
But tell me, does she want to move again? –

No.

– Does she want to work? –

No.

– What does she want to do least? –

Move. Thanks Dad,
unless something else comes striking
down from the blue I have my answer.
See what I mean when I say that
only fathers understand,
truly understand, their sons.

JULY 8

– But what about you, son? –

What about me?

– You've been so strong all these
years. Do you like your job? –

Not really.

– Then why do it?
I loved my job, loved fixing cars. –

I do it because at this point
in my life I can't afford to leave,
to start all over again.
I make a lot of money.

– But it's not enough money? –

No.

– I don't understand that. –

Well, we've gotten in over our heads,
I suppose, over the years,
buying furniture we shouldn't have,
TVs, stereos, computers,
going on vacations to Cape Cod and
Disneyworld.

– So where'd you get the money from? –

Borrowed it. Spent it when we really
didn't have it to spend.

– I don't believe that.
I never taught you to do that. –

I know you didn't, but
I guess I never listened to you.

– How could you have spent money
you didn't have? How could you not
have listened to me? –

I was only 15, Dad, when you died.
Remember?

(He looks at me, his face a frown
of dusty wrinkles.)
What do I do now?

– That's easy – Undo all the credit.
Get rid of it all,
all of it, and don't do it again, ever,
understand? –

Yes Dad.

JULY 9

– So you're doing a job only
for money. –

Well, yes.

– How could you have gotten
yourself into such a situation? –

It's a long story.

– I have time, plenty of time –

(I begin to cry. I don't
know why, but I
begin to cry uncontrollably, damn me.
My dad looks at me, sad,

waiting patiently for me to stop.
He touches my shoulder.)

– Go on –

In high school, Dad, after you'd
gone I had no one.

– there was Mom –

Oh, she was never very smart,
has always sort of had her
head in the sand,
fearful of confrontation, of
making decisions,
afraid of life . . .

– Don't talk about your mother
that way, don't! I won't
hear it. She did the best she could
given what she had. –

I'm sorry, you're right,
quite right. Sorry.

– well, go on –

The only thing I was good
at in high school was biology,

and the only teacher
who took any interest in me
whatsoever,
was Mr. Moyer, the biology teacher,
so I decided to major in
biology in college.

– to become a biologist –

Well, no.
To become a veterinarian.

– What? –

I had a part-time job in an
animal hospital, and
the veterinarian there
liked me, and I looked up to
him so, he was
smart and strong and honorable
and had lots of money and
hobbies and talents . . . .

– He inclined you towards
being a veterinarian. –

Right.

– So that's a good job and you
loved animals. I remember. –

Yes I did.
I loved them then, spent all my
Saturdays at the Staten Island Zoo.

– raised hamsters –

Kept snakes and frogs and lizards
and toads and tanks of turtles.

– Caught a couple of pigeons,
named them Mike, and what was the
other one, oh yes, Venus,
Venus the pigeon. You started
your own flock –

Oh God! (We laughed then, the
two of us; my birds flew off to
join a real flock
flapping around a few blocks away.)

I even wrote a book
you know, about tropical fish,
when I was only 17,
tried to get it published,
but,

we needed some money to put down,
a thousand dollars I think,
but we didn't have
any money.

(My dad was quiet then for
a long while, sitting
there, lightly rubbing his
forehead.)

– I didn't leave you any money
when I died. I just never
thought –

It's OK, Dad.
It's OK. ♣

Twelve Months

These pages are from a journal I kept while taking a graduate course in art therapy after the death of my first wife. Looking back, I think I was practicing what Dr. David Steindl-Rast called "openness for surprise," his way of saying what hope is really about.

James Sedwick

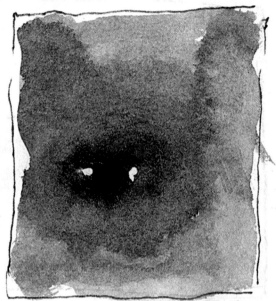

NOV. 1985: My wife died. In that darkness was (is) a new beginning for both of us.

DEC. 1985: I was lonely and cold. I started wearing flannel pajamas to bed!

JAN. 1986: The stir of new directions for me. Jan. 4, two months since her death, narcissus flowers open at my friend's house. My wife bought the flowers for us.

FEB. 1986: A difficult month — cold, lonely, and I got a miserable attack of flu. The depression and anxiety was great.

MARCH 1986: Four months to the day,
Mar. 4th, Marcella died. This anniversary
evening the oil lamp which she gave me
went out at 8:30 PM, the moment of her death!

APRIL 1986: My new directions, possibilities
of learning, I spend 3 days at
Kirkridge with the poet Robert Bly. The
center is on top of a mountain.

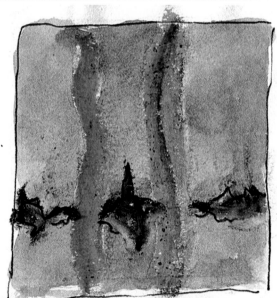

MAY 1986: May 4th, 6 month anniversary
of M's death, beautiful cactus flowers
open on a favorite plant of ours.

JUNE 1986: A busy month of learning
and doing. A red hybiscus flower
opened (the 1st) on our wedding anniversary.

JULY 1986: July 4th, 8 months after her death, I find a beautiful white columbine flower in front of my sculpture "White Seed" in my back yard.

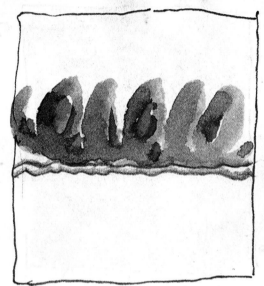

AUGUST 1986: A busy month of traveling and studying, with a little vacation at the end of the month near a river.

SEPT. 1986: Anxiety of starting school once again. Busy with reading, writing. Sept. 4th, 10 month anniversary, I discover pink rose on M's rose bush in backyard.

OCT. 1986: School work, other demands, new relationship— busy and anxious! But enjoying it!

Zebra Dream and Pear Pair

I was a 6-year-old navigating a No. 2 pencil between pale blue guidelines; an adolescent wielding a cartridge pen, filled with peacock blue ink, in a left-handed arc across the pages of a composition notebook; a young adult tapping the keys of an electric typewriter that slapped sepia letters onto crinkled vellum. Now in my fifties, I write journal entries on a laptop computer and print onto handmade papers that I layer with a life-long collection of found and original mixed media images. Journal pages are my diary and treasure map, the sanctuary where I endeavor to reconcile my introspective, stand-still-and-observe-the-splendor-of-the-ordinary life with my longing for adventure and experiencing the extraordinary. I've never seen a zebra in the wild, but I have discovered the wild zebra within myself. Journal pages remind me of the truth.

Deborah Arnold

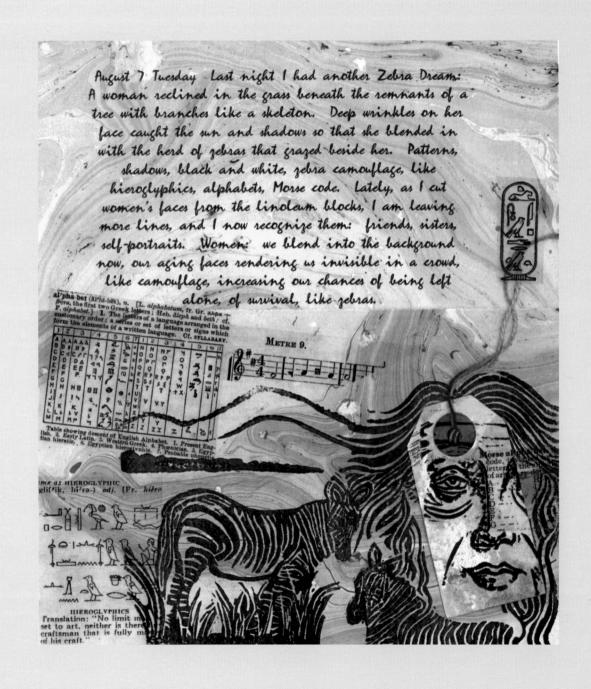

August 7 Tuesday Last night I had another Zebra Dream:
A woman reclined in the grass beneath the remnants of a
tree with branches like a skeleton. Deep wrinkles on her
face caught the sun and shadows so that she blended in
with the herd of zebras that grazed beside her. Patterns,
shadows, black and white, zebra camouflage, like
hieroglyphics, alphabets, Morse code. Lately, as I cut
women's faces from the linoleum blocks, I am leaving
more lines, and I now recognize them: friends, sisters,
self-portraits. Women: we blend into the background
now, our aging faces rendering us invisible in a crowd,
like camouflage, increasing our chances of being left
alone, of survival, like zebras.

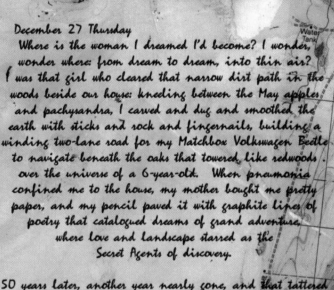

December 27 Thursday

Where is the woman I dreamed I'd become? I wonder,
wonder where: from dream to dream, into thin air?
I was that girl who cleared that narrow dirt path in the
woods beside our house: kneeling between the May apples
and pachysandra, I carved and dug and smoothed the
earth with sticks and rock and fingernails, building a
winding two-lane road for my Matchbox Volkswagen Beetle
to navigate beneath the oaks that towered, like redwoods,
over the universe of a 6-year-old. When pneumonia
confined me to the house, my mother bought me pretty
paper, and my pencil paved it with graphite lines of
poetry that catalogued dreams of grand adventure,
where love and landscape starred as the
Secret Agents of discovery.

50 years later, another year nearly gone, and that tattered
map of directions is folded and tucked in the drawer
beside my bed, the first page of a child's diary of living
an explorer's life, of grandeur beyond the weeding, the
laundry, the dishes, the homework, the bedtime prayers
that pleaded "If I should die before I wake, I pray Thee
Lord, my soul to take."

Now, I only travel in my sleep, and I pray not to wake
from the dreams in which I ride on a Zebra's back
while he canters across the savanna beneath
the blazing afternoon sun. I ride and ride and ride
until the sky is turquoise and vermillion, until
I'm at the edge of the horizon beneath a canopy of
midnight blue illuminated by God's Hope Dust. But just
like this morning, I awaken to my husband's snoring,
and the dogs whimpering for breakfast, and the
beep-beep-beep signaling the brew cycle is done and the
coffee is ready, and it's time to get up and begin
another ordinary day.

Zebra (Equus zebra).

Altocumulus stratiformis

August 2 Thursday Only two more days to finish the painting for the
"Just Pears" exhibition, and all I can think of is oranges, and the
unlikely orange grove in Tucson, at the Ghost Ranch Motel, where I chose
to stay because of the name (and the $39 a day rate during monsoon
season). The grove was an oasis amid the spare, utilitarian units.
Two rows of trees arched over a groomed gravel path and trellis, the
intense sun releasing a musty-sweet scent that filtered into the cool,
shaded haven beneath. An Orange grove in the Sonoran desert:
was it the sanctuary of someone homesick for someplace else?

Pears from the neighbor's trees are falling over our picket fence into
the blue rug junipers, attracting bees and squirrels and the dog – he
plays with them, tossing one into the air, then chasing its erratic
trail when it drops and rolls. Harvesting models will be easy, just say,
"Leo, fetch!" and I'll have the pear to use as inspiration for the painting,
pale lime green, with just a touch of orange.

ORANGE. 6s & 8s.

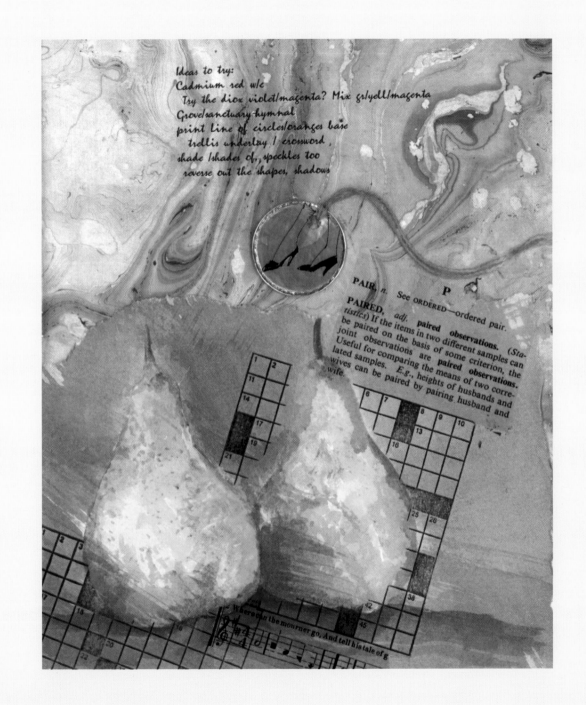

The Story of the Making of a YoYo Quilt

My usual mediums are etching, lithography, linoleum and woodcut. I am preoccupied with the theme of time, often expressed through light and darkness (color and black & white versions of a particular theme), or as a sequence of events.

I relate the YoYo Quilt to earlier Garden Journals, all of which are a series of small images of whatever caught my attention that day. The YoYo Quilt began with linoleum block prints of pieces of fabric, either in color or black and white. When I made a yoyo out of the fabric square by stitching a hem round the outer edge and pulling the thread, it created an immediate abstraction of what was a flower or a bird or a rabbit. However, because of my need for it to mean something, I look upon the black and white side of the quilt as the ocean evoking flashes of fire (or life) between the yoyos, and the color side as a large garden border evoking a feeling of air between the yoyos.

Ann Zahn

GARDEN JOURNAL XVI, THE YO YO QUILT
LINOLEUM CUT ON COTTON 6'x3' WALL HANGING
AUGUST 2007

I saw an old quilt of multi-colored rosettes in a museum on a Maine island. The caretaker told me how it was made. "You cut a 7 inch circle of cloth, stitch around the circle with large stitches, and pull the thread tightly. Knot it and you have a 'puff' or 'yoyo.'" Each yoyo has a puffed side and a smooth side.

SEPTEMBER

At my studio I began to make the yoyos out of old linoleum block prints done in color on old cotton sheets. I started sewing them together and my neighbor, who makes quilts, came over to see. "Oh," she said, "that's a yoyo quilt and I have a book with pictures and directions for making one." She said the yoyos usually alternate between "puff" and "smooth" so that both sides of the quilt are similar. So I alternated when I sewed them together, and kept printing and sewing more.

OCTOBER

My friend who next saw it said she much preferred the "puff" sides and, since I respect her judgment and agreed with her, I reversed all the smooth sides. This rearrangement took up the whole month.

NOVEMBER

Our artist daughter came to visit and looked at it and said, "WOW! I see black and white." I thought about this statement for a few days and got the idea of putting black and white yoyos on top of the diamond-shaped intervals between the colored yoyos. So I printed many black and white prints on new cotton, made yoyos and started sewing them over the diamond-shaped spaces between the colored yoyos. Since I had to lay the quilt on a table to do this, I couldn't see what the other side looked like. But I imagined the black and white smooth side would make the colored puff side rather wild!

DECEMBER

The black and white "puff" side of the quilt began to remind me of watching the sea, with sparkling waves of color, foam, and a constant rhythmic movement. I worked harder and harder to finish it so I could see the other side.

I finally got all the yoyos made and sewn, and hung the quilt up. Though it was poorly sewn together, I couldn't believe how mesmerizing the colored puff side was with the black and white diamond shapes peeking out.

I began to envision more "crazy" quilts – faces of friends and various animals on smooth yoyos, solid colors and abstract shapes on puffs and smooths, black and white words between colored puffs, mixing larger and smaller yoyos, et-cetera!

FEBRUARY: BOTH SIDES NOW

My neighbor, having noticed the poor sewing, returned and helped me sew the puffs so that many gaps in the quilt were filled in. I am finally beginning to see what I had envisioned in November. It begins to look like something I've never seen before, and I can't seem to stop sewing and looking at it.

 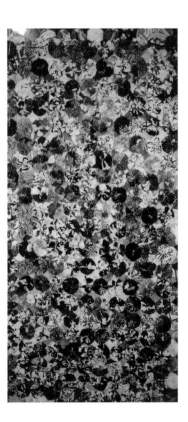

Pigeons in the Planter

In the summer of 2006, I watched a pair of pigeons raise their babies in a potted oleander tree on the terrace of our condo on a pier in downtown Baltimore.

One night my husband Andy called me to come and see two pigeons sitting on the railing of our terrace 20 stories above the harbor. They sat for a long time and looked like they were contemplating something important.

A week later I went to work in my studio, a sliding glass door away from the terrace, and discovered two eggs next to the tree in the blue planter.

In my work as a photographer, I have never taken the opportunity to photograph the same subject day after day, or rather minute by minute.

In this case it was really hard for me to leave the scene, ever.

Stephanie Graham

8/01/07   7:42 pm

Through July and August the parents took turns sitting on the eggs and caring for the babies. The father took the day shift and the mother the night.

8/02/07   8:15am

7/31/07   3:37pm

The babies went from smooth, dark, limp and fragile creatures, to little bodies armed with quills and finally to birds with feathers that I recognized.

8/09/07   12:40pm

I promised myself I wouldn't feed them but it was hard to resist the urge. I wanted to see if they'd open their mouths for me the way they did for their parents if I put my hand near their beaks. One very hot day on the terrace, they opened their mouths and I gave them water on my fingers (and took photos with my other hand).

In August I was away for two weeks. When I left they were still babies, snuggled up to each other. They would change positions, always touching, but they never left the pot. When I got back they were birds! They puffed up when I came near, like adolescents, showing attitude.

8/20/07   8:06pm

When all of the feathers were in and their wings were ready, they began to practice flying between the rim of the planter and the bench.

8/23/07   5:43pm

7/27/07   10:20pm

8/25/07 6:54pm

The babies went from eggs to flying birds in no time! And not just my two, but millions of pigeons all over the world. How could I have never noticed that incredible occurrence before in my life?

I'm glad I had a chance to keep looking at them. After two months (and more than 2800 pictures!) they weren't pigeons anymore.

1992

I Met the Old Man

As a poet, I use my journal as the place where I jot down words and ideas for safekeeping. When ordinary days resonate beyond the moment, I need to record them. In the journal, ideas can germinate and grow. It becomes a kind of savings account I can borrow from. The journal brings to mind the doomsday vault off the coast of Norway, where agricultural seeds are stored in case of worldwide catastrophe. In the journal, I collect the seeds of my best moments, in case I lose inspiration.

Robert Penn Warren said, "A lot of current can come through a small wire." It is my hope that the journal can serve as my small wire.

Sauci Churchill

SEPTEMBER 11, 1992

I met the old man at the bus stop today.

Having missed his bus, he wished he could transport himself to another place and be less annoyed. I told him about the book on shamanism. He has an elegant way of speaking, unusual in contemporary conversation. I try to string a juicier sentence for him.

I should bring in my plants. Walking home after work, I approach my buddleia bush covered with monarchs and dark swallowtails as welcome.

I love the way morning glories have overtaken the tomato plants. The effect is startling, red tomatoes smothered with violet blue flowers.

I dream of a flowery garden by the sea, littoral pools with their clicking sound, a small light-filled house by the sea.

Content, my dog pants by my side, her body against mine. ❧

1993

A Few Days in Bombay

When I travel, I always keep a journal. I need to bring back images as ephemeral as dandelion spores on a gusty day. Like photographs, but more important than pictures, are images that leap to mind with words written on the spot – the filtering grays of Mont-Saint-Michel on a November day, the Great Wall of China looping and curving over uneven terrain like a live serpent, aromas of the thronged marketplace of Marrakech at dusk, the uncanny sound of a Buddhist monk's horn, the taste of bouillabaisse in Collioure. I keep the journal around for a few months or years. Perhaps a poem, a story or a painting will emerge. The best, of course, is simply reliving those moments.

In the spring of 1993 my husband Robert MacDonald was invited by the Chamber of Commerce of the State of Andhra Pradesh, India, to address a meeting on how a state government conducts foreign trade. He had work to do; I explored Bombay on my own.

Louise Roberts Sheldon

MARCH 5, TAJ MAHAL HOTEL, BOMBAY

India is heaven! Everywhere I look I find a feast for the eyes, the oranges and lavenders of the flowers banked around our room, outside our window purple bougainvillaea, red hibiscus, yellow balls of mimosa brightening the gardens below. In the streets it's the women, their billowing saris, dyed every color of the rainbow and draped in a hundred ways, women streaming along sidewalks, intermingling in a moving mosaic of humanity. A man rides a motorcycle, his wife perched on God knows what behind him, clutching her doll-like children in their patent-leather shoes and sunglasses.

But India has its nether side as well. Does anyone besides me see the Dravidians? Those small people from the south with gray-black skin, the low-caste poor who work incessantly on the disintegrating streets of Bombay. Bedraggled women in filthy rags carrying rocks and cement in huge bowls on their heads to fix ruts and potholes made by nonstop traffic of hand-drawn cars, taxis, trucks and three-wheeled jalopies that have a penchant for turning over. One of the slender, dark women is quite beautiful, but no one notices because she's socially off the page, nonexistent.

In Mahatma Gandhi's house I read Gandhi's letter to Hitler, telling him that he didn't think war was a good idea. "My ambition is to wipe every tear from every eye," said Gandhi. He smiled in the face of his assassin, as he was shot three times, and forgave his murderer.

MARCH 6, DAY OF THE TEMPLES

When I call for a taxi, a great white vehicle resembling a 1935 Cadillac appears with a burly driver who speaks no English. I tell him one word, "TEMPLES." The man nods. He gets it. So I set out in the would-be Cadillac with the driver whose heavy hand on the horn hounds lesser contraptions to one side as it careens down the middle of the road. For a moment I relish the thought of commanding traffic, as though I were Queen Victoria. The car comes to a shuddering halt and the driver points to a set of steps that soar straight up over a jungle of houses and apartments.

"Babulnath," he says, wiping his black moustache with the back of his hand.

It is a daunting climb on a warm day, which brings me at the top to a shrine situated on a wide platform where a band of raucous urchins chase a soccer ball high over the roofs of the city below. Glancing around, I realize I should remove my shoes, thus allowing my feet to enjoy the refreshing coolness of the temple's inlaid marble floor. I enter a columned structure open to the air on three sides where a few people mill about among statues of various deities. Before me a devotee presents a bouquet of bright orange marigolds to a white-gowned priest for blessing. The holy man takes the flowers in his arms and with great ceremony places them on a sculptured image which I imagine to be Shiva from its ferocious look. Beside me, the paunchy elephant god Ganesh with his twisting trunk smiles rakishly under a wreath of pink hibiscus. Farther on a statue of Rama, the lion god, is being painted a vivid orange, not with a brush, but with a devotee's bare palm. A worshipper stretches out his hand to me in welcome. All at once, a feeling of lightness and happiness sweeps over me. In this intimate shrine I feel my presence is as natural as that of the murmuring doves, the chattering birds that nest in vines hanging from a trellis and the young boys bickering over their ball in front of the shrine. This is an India I can love.

As I descend the long stairway to the street, I come on an aperture from which the white faces of two brown cows observe me. Their necks are adorned with flowery garlands under welling eyes and soft ears that hang below their horns like pendant blossoms. From their satisfied expressions, I know they're convinced it's right that they be so revered. Yesterday I saw cows sleeping in the middle of a highway with no barriers; traffic roared by on both sides.

These animals are quite safe, of course, for it's worth a man's life to harm a sacred cow. We've noted many more sensibly tethered off the road, but none are as beautiful as the cows of Babulnath.

Mahalakshmi Temple was built centuries ago, jutting prominently over the sea on a grander scale than Babulnath. Three bundled women squatting under parasols before the temple vie for the privilege of guarding my shoes. I buy a bouquet of lavender lotus from a vendor clad in pink under her striped umbrella, then pull the chain of a brass bell hanging before the open temple to announce my presence. By now I know the drill. Lakshmi is the goddess of wealth. A handsome couple in red-and-green silk laced with jewelry of gold and precious stones presents the female deity with an assorted bouquet. Lakshmi and her two sister goddesses smile indulgently on their offering.

The ritual is not complete. I follow the young couple out on the rock ledge behind the temple where other worshippers are flinging their flowers, now properly blessed, onto the sea. Here a green wreath floats, there a pink lotus bobs happily on the waves, returned to nature after bringing good fortune to their bearers. Overhead I see three great vultures careening in the winds above the slender Tower of Merkala. Here I've been told Parsee devotees place the naked bodies of their dead, also to be returned to nature by the huge black birds. The tower is off-limits to the uninitiated.

Our third visit is to the Hari Krishna temple out by the airport. Set coolly in a grove of towering trees, its adjacent hotel is the seat of an ashram, a retreat for disciples of Hinduism. Young Europeans and Americans sprawl on balconies that encircle the residence, exchanging ideas, I suppose – or maybe pot. From the open verandas of the temple come haunting blasts of conch horns held by three half-naked priests, Michelangelesque in their sculptured brown masculinity. The temple's deep red color echoes the mournful sound, accompanied by a clamorous agitation of devotees' bells and a pungent aroma of incense.

On the street we note a vendor carrying an entire supply of kitchenware and utensils on his head. Another anomaly is the man casually throwing a sack, full of garbage, into the Indian Ocean in front of the lofty Gateway of India, that reminder of a hundred years of British rule.

MARCH 11

What a fine vegetarian luncheon with Raka Sanakar and Barat Doshi, who have decided to entertain me while Bob is busy. A sumptuous and spicy repast served in small bowls, eaten with fingers and by dipping bread, and giving off a melee of aromas! I recognize cinnamon, cardamom and turmeric, but there are many others. Mr. Doshi, being an ascetic Jain, eats no meat, eggs, fish or poultry. Nor does he eat potatoes or other vegetables grown underground. Despite these deprivations Mr. Doshi, whose family has been Jain for centuries, is genial and full of jokes. When undecided, he rolls his head in a circle, the very image of the saucy elephant god, Ganesh. Raka wears a purple sari and is in good humor, though she is fasting and eats nothing. We visit the cool white marble temple where twenty-four Jain gods greet us. Jain devotees wear white masks to prevent their inhaling and thus killing insects. So many injunctions, so many rules to live by! But my hosts are in no way depressed. Only when I reach my room, riding on a high despite the fireworks in my stomach, do I know why hotel guests have been staring at me. I'm wearing a huge red smear on my forehead, the sign of a Jain.

MARCH 12, DUBBED "BLACK FRIDAY" IN FUTURE EDITIONS OF THE BOMBAY PRESS

My husband is off again early to meetings, luncheon and a conference. I plan to cruise the Colaba shopping area, but am stopped at the hotel door. A bomb has gone off in the Bombay Stock Exchange. Forty have been killed! The concierge has no further information; guests are advised to stay in the hotel.

In my room I listen to television news of more explosions in Bombay. Bob comes in and I hug him. "Need a few papers. Later I'll be at the Air India Building," he says, dashing out. Half an hour later on BBC I see an explosion – it's the spanking new Air India building flying in pieces through the air. He couldn't have been in the building! He said "later." I've learned to be stoic, but I can't sit in that room any longer. I go downstairs to an art show that has just opened.

The artist Bulbul Singh is a tall, dark man with chiseled features. I find his soft, pastel-colored abstractions in oil interesting, but I am especially intrigued by selections of Singh's poetry in English placed alongside each painting. Not bound by the conventions of a mother tongue, he strings together words in startling, refreshing groupings. A friend of the artist bursts in suddenly to say there have now been four bombings, the dead are being shoveled out of the Air India building. The blasts may be attributed to a fundamentalist Hindu group. Or to Muslims who object to a Hindu shrine on the site of a destroyed Muslim shrine, which was built on an earlier Hindu site. I continue to read the poems. Singh's words are soothing and help me forget what's going on. We make nervous chitchat about his art. I like Bulbul Singh, an overage hippie, an idealist with a way with words. He tells me I remind him of an American he once met.

"In those days we used to sit around talking about the emptiness of our lives, when we had everything in the world, everything material, that is. We were the 'beat generation,' leftovers of the sixties movement. Four of my buddies came with me to a retreat in the mountains." Bulbul Singh now lives in the Himalayas where he's teaching villagers how to grow apples and has set up a school for children.

I ask whether his friends are still with him in his mountain retreat.

"No way! The others have abandoned the high altitudes, and our lofty ideals which they now consider crazy, for domestic happiness and children. The Americans went back of course when the U.S. economy sagged and travelers' checks stopped coming in."

"But you're still here," I said.

"Can you believe I started a meditation class among the villagers? It's already helped them. For one thing alcoholism is way down. And that nightmare the caste system – I'm working on that, too."

"I'd like to know how," I said skeptically, thinking of the beautiful Dravidian carrying a bowl of cement on her head.

"It's no joke. The village upper crust refuses to make contributions for animal sacrifices that are a part of normal village ritual. So I throw some money in the pot to make up for them. I make money with my paintings! Anyway, it's a way to keep peace!"

I go back to our room. No Bob. I turn on the TV. Within four hours there have been fourteen explosions in Bombay, many in hotels. People are dead all over the city. I think of the mayhem in the streets and the anguish of families. The artist speaks of a way to keep peace. Peace for whom? Where is Bob? On what street? In what building?

Moments later, a knock on the door. I rush to find Bob – unscathed! His appointment with Air India had been postponed. A miracle! How lucky we have been so many times in so many places!

Reluctantly we call off our dinner at the Doshi home. Everyone is too upset by the bombs. BBC tells us that two hundred and five have been killed, one thousand wounded. No group has claimed responsibility for the massacre. What does this mean for India?

A blip in the millennia of its history? Or the start of some larger conflict between Hindus and Muslims? Between India and its neighbor Pakistan?

We grieve for India and make plans to move on. ♣

1995

Raising Senara

My daughter, Senara, was born as I was finishing graduate school, and my friends humorously dubbed my dissertation "Raising Senara." The dissertation was actually a book of poems about how the women in my family connected through the generations, and although I did not use their suggestion for my title, it ultimately became the title of a journal I kept for my daughter.

The first seven pages of her journal were written when she was between the ages of two and three years old. It was a difficult time for both of us as I was separating from her father and learning how to be a single mother.

Senara turned 15 years old on January 7, 2008. I have kept the journal for her all these years, writing in it several times per year recording memories that make us laugh, smile and reflect as we both grow and change, sometimes dancing and sometimes stumbling through our lives.

Rosalie Sanara Petrouske

MAY 28

Senara is almost three years old. When she was very small, premature and first home, she would clear her throat, and the noise she made sounded like the cries of a baby dolphin. "She is going to be quite vocal when she grows up," the nurses in the Special Care nursery predicted. She is, of course, constantly talking to her dolls or to herself. She is interested in the world around her and still maintains her fascination from last summer with the moon. At night when we drive out, she looks for the white globe in the sky and sings *oh, moon, moon, moon.* From the time she has started to talk, her words have been clear, each syllable enunciated perfectly, and instead of speaking in garbled baby sentences, she uses articles and conjunctions. Yesterday, we traveled to a waterfall, and Brian, my friend of 16 years, showed her the miniature pinecones breaking open, explained that pine trees came from the cones, opened one that was bursting with a tiny bud of green life. We showed her maple leaves, smaller now than her hand. Spring comes so late to these northern woods. We watched a mother robin feeding her babies in a nest snuggled high in a poplar tree, and taught her how to be quiet, to wait for a chipmunk to emerge from a hole in a hollowed-out tree stump. She bent gently over a carpet of blue wood violets, so startlingly blue in the emerald grass, and did not pick one as we told her not to. Brian, now 33 and so tall and dignified from the boy I knew at 19, stopped next to Senara, held her palm to a bed of moss growing at the foot of an old pine. "Isn't this soft? Just like a blanket?" he asked her. She nodded solemnly, already beginning to revere nature.

DECEMBER 11

I love my daughter so much, but sometimes she makes me angry. It is the independence in her that angers me; the insistence that she must do everything herself. When she washes her hands or brushes her teeth, she does not want me to help her. It is the same thing with washing her hair. She wants to pour her own shampoo over her wet curls, and then she empties the whole bottle into the bathwater. This summer she wanted to climb the slide by herself, pulled herself up the metal bars of the jungle gym, kicked and screamed when I climbed up to catch her. "Leave me alone," she said. She is daring. At daycare, she walks the balance beam and at home leaps from the bed to the floor. She loves to be turned upside down, to swing in circles until she is too dizzy to walk straight, giggles uncontrollably when her father tosses her into the air. She has no fear of heights or falling, or running out into the street. She is a gymnast, a climber, a skydiver. I think I recall this from my own childhood. I was the nine-year-old who loved to hang from a trapeze bar until the summer evening I fell straight down, my head snapped back into my shoulders and I could not breathe. My grandmother, who was picking bellflowers by the front porch, turned me upside down and pounded my back until my breath came back in one long scream. That was the end then, of my daring, of thinking I was immortal. Perhaps I was lucky I did not break my neck, but in a way I became one kind of cripple. It is one thing to be careful, another to be so careful you stop yourself from flying. I want Senara to fly, but not too far away, too soon.

MAY 28, 1996

It has been a long winter; a record winter for snow, ice and cold. There are still remnants of ice floes in the bay and Lake Superior remains gripped in winter's hungry grasp. Stores are selling T-shirts depicting a snowman hanging in a noose. "Survivor, Winter of 96," the front of the shirt proclaims. It has been a difficult winter for Senara and me, emotion and mother-guilt ruling our lives. Senara fights me with her three-year-old wisdom and strong independence for such a small person. I have lost friends, and a job, and love. It has been hard for me to understand that she is only a child, not old enough to bear the burden of adult grief and loss of faith. She counts to 20, she can point out the right street to turn down to take us home, back to the blue house on Harkin's Hill, her first home, the place of her conception. It has been confusing for her to have a mommy who cries all the time, who screams out her pain, who copes so poorly with any kind of loss. Now, finally the leaves have slowly unfurled. Their green encompasses the window frame and soon we will not be able to see out to the lake, once the leaves burst with hugeness. The wind still cuts at ears and cheeks when we walk by the cove, but a robin comes to the birdfeeder and tulips are blooming in gardens and along sidewalks. We read her books, *Millie, the Lop-Eared Rabbit, Scupper, the Sailor Dog, Poky Little Puppy*, and play with blocks or pick dandelions. I have the hours now, without a job, to do small domestic chores like dishes and spaghetti, and not feel cheated out of my precious time. When I am sad, Senara tells me, "It's all right, Mommy." She is like a wise old prophet in a shrunken body. I love her so much. My tousled haired, brown-eyed, skinned-kneed, dancing little girl. We will survive.

NOVEMBER 15

Fall came this year with color so startling it throbbed across the landscape. At first, the leaves were slow to peak but then the red was brilliant, and after all that red the last leaves to fall were the yellows: burnt gold, daffodil spring yellow, warm butter yellow, cat-eye yellow, fool's gold yellow. I walked with my daughter outside into curtains of yellow, waterfalls of yellow, yellow leaves around our feet, falling in our hair, leaves delicate as the stems of slender crystal goblets. After our long, hard summer, I fear cold again, white of the snow, and being alone with my daughter, without her father. My heart has hardened. Sometimes I go through a week without any pain. One day I woke up to a sad song on the morning radio and cried until I was choking. But my tears are dry now and I feel myself slipping away into the void, the cavern that is frightening because anything can happen here. There is the small uplift of excitement that embracing change brings, but also it is like getting ready to jump from a plane . . . the fear of that first step into thin air, and then dropping away with only your chute to save you, to billow out behind you. Senara is more at peace now. She plays quietly sometimes with her books and her Legos, her dolls and stuffed bears. We laugh together, read books, tickle each other. At night, she has been my comfort, my warmth. I hold her curled sleeping body against the curve of my stomach and we sleep like the unborn still in the watery womb world. For that little time, we are safe and pure in our love, holding back the cold, holding back the winter in our hearts.

WEDNESDAY, JANUARY 1, 1997

Today is the first day of another new year. Senara took a late nap yesterday so at 11:30 p.m., she was wide awake. I dressed her in her coat and snow pants, and we walked downtown to watch the lighted ball on top of the clock tower drop. It was a warm night with banks of fluffy snow glinting in the blue moonlight. There were quite a few college students yelling, laughing and pushing, probably walking down from parties to see the ball drop. There were also many couples. Next to us stood a man and woman. He had a champagne bottle and when the ball started to drop, he popped the cork and kissed his girl. It felt weird being all alone, well, not really alone because I had Senara. I told her she was supposed to kiss me so she pressed her mouth against my cheek and kissed me twice. We left the merry group of people behind and started the walk home with me pulling Senara in her plastic sled. People drove by with their windows down and yelled "Happy New Year!" We walked by the house built by Hiram Burt, the one where Will Adams lived. Will Adams wrote an opera when he was in his early twenties and later died from a strange disease that left him paralyzed from the neck down. People said he was "the man who turned to stone." I like to think Will is a ghost who still sits on the long veranda staring out to Superior on warm summer days. I have told Senara this story so when we walk by and she hears pigeons cooing under the dormers, she thinks it is Will sighing for all the things he has missed as the centuries slowly slip away. She asked me what a ghost was, and I tried to explain. "You can't see or touch a ghost," I said, "but you can feel their sadness. A ghost doesn't have a body or wear clothes. If you put out your hand to touch one, your hand will slide through the air," I told her. "A ghost is someone who still wants to live in this world and experience all the things they never had the time to do. That's why Will stayed behind, watching the lake slowly pass by, the seasons come and go, and if you are very quiet and listen," I said, "you can hear him sighing softly like the sound of the wind in an oak tree." So tonight as we pass by, I wonder if Will is in the tower looking out at the snowy night and the silvery lake, listening to the laughter of people along the street as they welcome in another new year. Last night, I felt Will's friendly presence walking home with Senara and me, riding on the thin thread of laughter as my little girl bounced in her plastic saucer sled. ♣

1998

5 a.m. Journal: I wonder about emptiness . . .

I spent a few years waking up at 5 a.m. each day to write. I wanted to journal, but I didn't want to talk about my days as much as to reach inside myself, so I used a technique described by Natalie Goldberg: I remember, I don't remember; I know, I don't know; I see, I don't see. I wrote for 10 minutes using a simple prompt, and then 10 minutes on the opposite of that prompt. I was often surprised by what came out of the "opposite" prompt. I felt like I had found an entrance into the underside of things. This was my daily practice. I wrote from a space between two worlds, not thinking, just riding a wave, staying with the force at the foamy white curled edge of my experience.

Sindee Ernst

NOVEMBER 12

I wonder about emptiness. When words can't find an edge of meaning. When a stomach calls silently in loneliness and sorrow. I wonder if the moon knows she is in motion or that her light is blue. I wonder if the birds are glad to be flying south. If their wings shout back to them or if they just travel because traveling is what they know, or if they know what they know. Or if that would make a difference. I wonder if the young girl I was held some knowledge of a future. This future. If I held it and made it happen or if some external force like the wind or air or the continents moving, pressed hard against me moving me upwards and into my own life. I wonder about the state of being of a young child, of the balance between consciousness and this kind of flowing motion of days. I feel my old thoughts like exclamation points. When I am an adult I will never. I remember the things I thought I'd always remember and understand. I believed that if I said them out loud like promises I would be sure to create them. I did not know that there were things I didn't know yet. Like now, there are things I don't know yet but it is hard to take steps with that knowledge wrapped around you so you go forward anyway and sometimes you just can't look down. Marching. I wonder about the air the way it changes cold to warm and a day that keeps passing by. I wonder about the sickness in my throat that keeps me coughing. The sickness in me that touches my throat, my voice, is it telling me to be careful with how I speak. Or it is just there. Are all of our moments imbued with meaning or are we just flying south because it is in our grain. Our grain like the wood it gives a picture, a cross section of growth past and future, you look at that and see a journey. Trajectory. We are headed in some direction but we have feet and legs and this incredible ability to turn around and face a different direction, to throw our head back and look up at the sky, our arms out and twirl in any way, we have choice. I have choice.

I don't wonder if I will go the right way. There is only one way, as much as there are many ways, the one way is the way we go and it is always right. I don't wonder about the future it comes in inches and miles it comes at a warped speed, lights flickering on every side it hangs out there in the universe. I don't wonder about waking up inside of me, about the light that shines. I don't wonder about things scientific, about weather or chemistry and structure, I am willing to accept the truths that delight others but not me and know that they are just momentary truths. Most truths are that way. Little anchors to set in stone or sand to hold us guide us in our own storms the belief itself like gravity. For one day maybe that truth will change and we will find that the earth is round, didn't they just look up at the moon to imagine that these places floating in the sky were round. The sphere so obvious if you are looking at it. I don't wonder about how the air fills my lungs and feeds my blood. I am willing to trust that, too. I don't need to know all of this. I don't wonder about the old friends. The ones I haven't seen in too many years to count, the ones whose names are forgotten. Only the ones from kindergarten because I have an old strip of photos, school photos, with the teacher first, a teacher who looks absolutely and completely unfamiliar to me. And then the children, one by one, smiling photo smiles and I do remember them because I can see their future because I knew them for the years that followed. And more than others, I wonder about them and who they are and why for those short years or year our lives intersected, if there is meaning to that that we'll never know, if a word or a glance took our feet and turned them ever so slightly in a new direction. I don't wonder much about the teacher, who probably had the most direct impact at the time. There is no mystery in all of that directness. I don't wonder about the school or building then new now seeming old and tired, or maybe refurbished over the years but still with noisy fluorescent lights that buzz when you aren't noticing and are quiet when you want to fix them. I don't wonder about the person who took all of those pictures either. ❧

2000

Twyla Tales

My lack of understanding of what it takes to raise a baby, any baby, could best be summed up by something I said at my wife's baby shower when some toy was opened. "That'll buy you five minutes." Every eye focused on me and Lynn Sheridan said very precisely, "Five minutes is a long time." I felt properly embarrassed and chastised but didn't think anything of it. Now I know exactly what Lynn meant. Five minutes with a screaming newborn is an eternity. Multiply that by several hours and your brains turn quickly into runny eggs. Conversely five minutes of entertainment buys a lot – a heaven sent opportunity to shower or fix and eat lunch.

The two things I have pondered over and over now that our baby Twyla is pushing furniture around the house and beginning to climb up and open things like the knife drawer, etc., are – How does any kid live past the age of five? And how does any marriage survive kids?

Richard Peabody

SEPTEMBER 18

Twyla vs. The Bottle is ongoing. On Monday, Margaret went to work at about 9 a.m. after spending a little couch time with Twyla. So, I played with some of Twyla's Fisher-Price toys that are all sounds and movement. Did a little Jolly Jumper time. Life was good for half an hour and then Twyla flipped out at about 10 a.m. and screamed herself asleep. She napped for half an hour. Woke up screaming. I fed her about 2 ½-oz of rice cereal. She eats it just fine if you let her grasp the spoon. (She's a total control freak.) Twyla sits on the kitchen floor in her bouncy chair and I mix the gruel in a blue bowl and then spoon some. She'll wave the spoon off and then she'll open her mouth, and as I go to plop it in there, she'll grab the spoon with her left hand and guide my hand. Hilarious. She gets about half of it down. And she seems fine. Not even very messy.

We do that for half an hour, positioned so Twyla can watch her favorite trees – the two poplars with leaves flipping around all silver showy in the breeze. She seems content. I hand her the little Pooh sippy cup she likes, the one that cost a couple bucks at the grocery store, nothing like the other high priced top of the line bottles and cups and alternative feeding devices we've spent all of our money on, and because she can grasp both handles she'll pop it into her mouth. Sadly, she can't hold it high enough to get any milk out of it yet; so I kind of nudge the cup up a little higher and let gravity do its thing. This works for about an ounce. Wow. I get these coy little shy smiles, where Twyla turns her head to her right and hides her face in the chair fabric and then opens her mouth a little bit more when I praise her and hold up the spoon again. This isn't even really hard work. She likes eating. This is fun.

And then of course she goes sky high out of nowhere and starts screaming. I know she expects Mom to walk in the room any second and just can't figure out where she's gone. So I rock her and sing "Yellow Submarine" another 500 times, and bounce her on my knee, and try every teething ring and toy we own, and she tosses them to the floor with disdain, screaming all the while.

I should point out here that I mean screaming full blast right in your ear. Let me give you an example. Twyla received her four month shots a few weeks ago (she's 4 1/2 months old now), and everything was fine with the examination until our Doc left and the Nazi Nurse came in with the little plastic tray. She set that on the counter and Twyla's eyes locked on it the moment she heard the tiny clank. She could see the four needles. She looked at the tray, looked up at the Nazi Nurse, and then turned her head wildly to the right and fixed on me before she began screaming. (Amazing. She actually remembered the needles from the second month shots.) My wife demanded that I hold one leg, too, so Twyla would hate us both equally for this pain. Which I did. And felt like Dr. Mengele.

So, after another hour or so of Twyla's unabated screaming, at which point I'm positive Child Welfare people will knock on the door any moment and arrest me, she finally sacks out. It's amazing to watch. One second she's awake and the next in mid-scream her head nods over and she's gone. I watch for breathing cuz I always figure she just burst an artery or something. But no, my sweet little angel baby is asleep on the couch with me. Exhausted I nap too. For two hours. That's unprecedented. I'm almost refreshed. And then she wakes screaming. Nothing works. We try cereal again and fail. We try the bottle. We try the sippy cup. *Nada.* So I put on the Beatles again. That calms her. I walk her outside under the trees. I walk her around the yard.

But she won't let me stop. I have to keep moving. Can't even slow down to catch my breath.

Now I know what Phil Spector meant by a "Wall of Sound". And I also know why Rock and Roll was created – to drown out screaming babies.

At 4 p.m. I give up. I'm so fried, so tired, so sick of singing "Yellow Submarine," that I call my wife and say something cordial like "I quit." That's it. No please, no begging. Miss T. manages to scream during the entire wait and my wife finds us on the screen porch a half hour later (she took a cab) where my knee is on automatic and my eyes glazed over so much that I just hand the kid off and disappear down into my basement lair where I crank up really loud rock and roll for three hours. It takes me that long to right my sinking ship. Just as long to have an appetite again.

Margaret spends the rest of the evening wondering what "I quit" meant. Today? Forever? Being principal daycare provider? Being a father?

SEPTEMBER 19

I have finally admitted defeat. As much as I want to be a house poppa and take care of Twyla every single moment of every single day while my wife's bringing home the bacon. The truth is I can't handle it. I'm stressed out, still in a lot of pain from my back, super glad I'm not teaching right now, and beaten down. So after a lot of discussion it so happens that Fern Lawrence, who runs a nanny share out of Margaret Blair and Roger Connor's first floor almost across the street from our old house and looks like she plays basketball for the Mystics, has an opening. She watches four kids. Lizzie Connor, and Sara and Zach Danik. But Maria is taking Julia home because she's quitting and becoming a stay-at-home mom. We feel like we're giving our kid away to gypsies. I haven't felt this defeated in a long time. I've been upset and angry and flailing out in every direction and leaving Twyla with somebody else seems like a huge personal failure. I feel like I'm not worthy of being a father.

Anyway, today was great, cuz I'd had a rough night watching my stupid football team implode like choking dogs on national television. One of the worst losses to the hated Cowboys I've seen in my life. But hey, maybe I should call Dan Snyder, and take Twyla down to Redskins Park tomorrow. A couple hours of Twyla treatment and they'll play better. I know they will. ♣

1999

My Father's Last Years

My father was a bona fide cowboy. One of the last of the breed. He had always told me that if he could, he would die on a bed on stilts the Indian way, in a secluded spot in the canyon of his beloved ranch. We both knew that was impossible; however, I vowed to him that I would do all in my power to see that he died in his own home.

Through stumbling down the road paved with my proverbial good intentions to care for my father, I learned a lot about my relationship with him and gained a better understanding of his 62-year marriage to my mother, and her own struggle to find personal fulfillment.

As they say, growing old isn't for wimps; neither is caring for aging parents. I hope that by having chronicled the years I cared for my father, some modicum of wisdom may be handed down to those of my children and grandchildren who may face the same choices in the future.

Jennie L. Winter

Back home on the Weippe Prairie. Gene gone to work. Did few min. on Nordic track to get heart rate up. Put belly dance tape on and rattled things around for a while. Vivaldi CD on now. Contrast with radio report from Jaspar TX. Visualizing vividly black man being dragged on the end of a log chain for three miles. How can I process that and Vivaldi at the same time. Turned off radio. Hearing Vivaldi's cello's deep undercurrent of bass melody (*Summer*) Concerto No. 3 in G minor. 1. *Allegro non molto* – the end of *Summer* seems almost an accompaniment to that awful end of life and the undoubtedly gleeful racist pigs whose cruelty was a celebration of their hatred.

Gene remarked the other day how the town decided to remove the wrought iron fence between the white and black sections of the graveyard afterwards. We wondered together why it took such violence to achieve a common burial ground. How long chains have robbed black people of their lives. What a metaphor for the darkest depths of the white man's soul. A heavy chain of hatred that drags at our heels. Vivaldi is the imagined good – here today in the silence of the Weippe Prairie where *The Four Seasons* follow one another passionately, contemplatively, violently, peacefully; like life. Thank God for Vivaldi today and always.

MARCH 2

Headed for Pocatello again. This has been going on since 1995, gradually my visits to care for Dad have been getting longer and longer. Flying Horizon Air. Kinda bumpy. Dad was almost incoherent on the phone talking about his dad, his brothers, chickens, horses, etc. Totally confused. I hope not totally because out of the gibberish he said, "I sure love you, honey." I'm so afraid for him. I hope his mind returns to normal. He's been having these strokes, TIAs they call them. These awful calls. I remember when I called my mother on April 19, 1985 and she sounded much the same. I told her to get to the doctor, but she didn't. They called an ambulance for her at 9:00 p.m. Suffered for 19 days before she died from massive stroke. Can't get over that she was kept alive on respirator, fed by tube. Technology speeds ahead while people tag along behind like poor relations. That won't happen to Dad. (She said.)

MARCH, 1999

When I arrive home, Dad is worse than I expected. He greets me eagerly, hobbling out from the living room. His hair is too long, disheveled, and he is without his teeth. He smells bad. I am shaken to say the least. How frail and foolish he seems, whimpering out the fear that he will die if he goes to sleep. His strong hands seem feminine, their nails long and tapered. They flutter in the air like birds while he stammers out his apologies. "I know I'm a nuisance." I try to comfort him with the kind of contradictory humor we've used over the years to quell self pity. "Sure you are. Why don't you shape up?" I say lightly, but this time it doesn't work. My banter isn't followed by the usual grin. "Oh, Jennie, I won't live 'til morning. There's nothing they can do for me. I know it's cancer." I realize that Dad is truly afraid this time. I think of a line from King Lear:

You must bear with me
pray now forget and forgive
I am old and foolish . . .

It is hard to think of my father the protector being afraid of dying. I tell him that I can't stand to see him afraid. That he has always been fearless to me. Besides, I tell him, you aren't dying. You don't have cancer. He refuses to accept this. "You just don't know."

No sooner do I get to sleep than he is calling out again. Having a new baby was never so demanding. He has to have food, water. I empty his urinal time after time and try to persuade him that he needn't drink so much. "I have to keep everything working or I'll die. You see it's my prostate. I have to keep my bladder working."

MARCH 23

Took Dad to the doctor and he gave me some Atavan for Dad to alleviate his anxiety. I hate to give it to him, but the smallest effective dose has done wonders. I can finally sleep. Finally figured out why Dad thinks he's convinced he has cancer. Seems his best friend, Ernie, has recently passed away from prostate cancer. I'm trying to get him back to normal. Today he watched a Lawrence Welk rerun. This brings back memories of the times he watched Welk with Mom. He remarked several times about certain songs that Mom used to sing when they lived in the old house and were extremely happy with what was coming their way. Several times he calls me "Virgie." He corrects himself immediately, but it makes me think of all that she gave up for him. How she devoted most of her life to his. No wonder he is so helpless now. He puts his head down and covers his eyes with his hands. I read to him. "Do not go gentle into that good night . . ." It bewilders him when I burst into tears in the middle of it. He has no more capacity to rage against his old age. He is 90. Today is my birthday. 62 years old. Ha! On the downhill slide and picking up speed.

MAY 15

Haven't had much time to write. Living in a kind of *déjà vu*. Trying to make things young again in the yard and inside the house. Built a little rock wall and planted a bed of flowers around Dad's old horse-drawn plow. Found rusty horseshoes, rusting ax, an old hackimore, and hung them on the handles of the plow. Trying to make things the way Mom had them. Growing in my understanding of the deep sadness I remember seeing in my mother's big dark eyes. Finding small slips of paper with poems on them tucked away here and there. And the words to songs "I'm forever blowing bubbles," . . . "I've looked at life from both sides now." Poems she has written herself. Most reflect a personal lack of fulfillment. More each day, I realize how my father, steeped in the male hierarchy of his generation, had required her to give up so much of herself. One poem in particular about a country woman who bought a red dress. When her husband saw it he ridiculed her, saying that she had no use for a dress like that. So she put it into the back of her closet and never wore it. I think my Mom's "closet" was probably full of those metaphorical red dresses.

JUNE 5

Dad has something called "dumping syndrome" that demands that he eat small meals every two hours. He heard the doctor tell me that he shouldn't be left alone anymore. He now thinks that if I leave him for a few minutes he will surely die. Lord have mercy.!!!!!

JUNE 21

Not much change. I'm listening to Bach tonight. It is getting late. Gene called. Love to hear from him. I know he needs me to come home but won't say it because he feels that Dad is a priority right now. What a guy. I should take Dad home, but it would have to be kicking and screaming. Should be with my husband. Irony is I know that Dad would never have let my mom do what I am doing. I call my mom an "earth mother." She was that before the hippie culture picked it up. I wonder if she knew of her importance to the lives of all her children.

> *The smallest wave from the salt cellar*
> *reveals to us*
> *more than domestic whiteness;*
> *in it we taste infinitude.*
> Pablo Neruda

I think my mother, who never even learned to drive, had her place of importance in this world and the next. Like salt, she was important. Real important.

JULY 16

Phillip called today and paid me one of the nicest compliments I could wish for. He said that he had seen a beautiful sunset and that it reminded him of me. That is what I mean by the metaphor of teaching my children and students "rainbows" and "wild Roses" – the earth and her beauty and how much we are a part of it. I am so glad that my firstborn son, indeed all my children, understand this and live as close to the earth as they can.

JULY 19

I think I know why women keep plants in pots. I know it was my mother's and my own way of getting through the long winters alone. Those little plots of mother earth were such a comfort when they nourished geraniums, ivy, Christmas cactus, wandering Jew and even such exotics as begonias and African violets. And I miss the root cellars of days gone by which were dug-outs with lumber and earth roofs over them. They, too with their rows of fruit and veggies and bins of root vegetables were a testament to the power of the earth to protect and nurture – a reminder that a cold winter can be survived much as we survive any other harsh fact of life. Always there is the promise of the good sweet earth and the overarching rainbow. Does the simple act of tending a plant in a pot teach a child to nurture a parent? Gotta give my daughters and sons an ivy or something. What goes around comes around. I'm looking at my mother's and father's fate and seeing my own some day. Shakespeare said it, *Thou art thy mother's glass . . .*

AUGUST 10

Dad can't really say it, but I know that he is embarrassed. I know he hates that I have to help him with his every function. I have to help him get on and off the commode and to support him and help him stand to use his urinal. He can't urinate when he lies down or sits. He has always been such a modest man and it does seem cruel that I should have to see his behind and his privates just because he's getting old and sick. I remember when his mother died. I was with Grandma when the nurses came in to turn her over and make her bed. They didn't show much appreciation of her modesty, because I saw her bare bottom and the gray pubic haired private parts. I hated them for that. I don't know what it is about our bodies that the part that produced us is so ugly; especially when we grow old. I tried to put him in diapers, but he takes them off and throws them on the floor. Last night when I glanced in to check on him his penis was hard and stretched out in front where he lay sleeping on his side on the edge of the bed. I was shocked and saddened that he would still have that sort of nighttime experience when he is so old and alone. Probably a strange take on that experience, but I felt that he had not long to go before his death. I feel that way often, though. Depression I guess. I've watched my father grow old and enter another country. A place where things have faded before his eyes then almost disappeared due to macular degeneration. Familiar sounds have faded; the body that was strength for others has weakened and shrunk, until he can't care for this own needs. And I am pretty much alone in the gravity of this occurrence. The old saying that one man can provide and care for 10 children, but 10 children can't take care of one parent, seems true. I've been trying my best, but right now I feel that I can't go much longer with the kinds of problems I am faced with in Dad's daily care unless I have help from the rest of the family. I can't lift him, I have trouble feeding him the right things – his appetite has gone bye bye. And I hate to empty a pot full of poop. I'm doing it, though. I guess that I really can do it, then.

JANUARY 30, 2000

The holidays are over. Dad enjoyed a Thanksgiving and Christmas at home, and many of his children came to visit. Lots of work, but truly delightful time for all. Much personal soul searching has gone into my decision to continue to take care of my father. But I am tired. My marriage is a distant memory almost. I have heard from almost all my brothers that I should put Dad in a nursing home and give up. I'm so afraid that he will die like Mom did, alone and sick. I wonder if any of them or myself included can fully understand the meaning of the word sacrifice. With the supreme sacrifice of the Savior in mind, I've come to the conclusion that becoming able to give of one's self purely and with understanding and compassion is imperative if our existence is to count for anything. Sacrifice is the prime mover in our lives. I see the connotative meaning of "sacrifice" in the rich, velvet verb "nurture". The two words name that which makes possible our existence as beings capable of progressing to a higher realm. Yet, in reading these words over, I realize how many times fatigue of body and mind have collided suddenly with my best and purest intentions. It makes me wonder why I even try. Perhaps true sacrifice begins with the first pangs of pain that one ignores in order to do for someone else. But sometimes I wonder if it is wrong to nurture my father when he is so old and his future is so limited. Who am I to try to determine the mission of a man. Who am I to question my place in eternity or in the life of this man who is my father at this time and in this place. Choices are there to be made. The way I live with them is the way I will regard myself. I must believe that what I'm doing will prove to be right – to have moved both my father and me forward. I pray every night that it is so.

FEBRUARY 17

I had to do it. I didn't wait for help from any of my brothers. I told Dad
that I had found an assisted living home for him where about eight other
gentlemen were living. I can't get his wheelchair around in this little house,
and I found out that when he goes down, even though I am wearing a belt, I
can only break his fall and it is extremely difficult to get him back on his feet.
He seemed to understand, but when I had him ready to get in the front seat
of my car, he suddenly took hold of both sides of the door and said, No! It
almost broke my heart. I took him back inside and told him that he had no
choice, that I had to go home for awhile and there was no one else to care for
him. I told him I understood how hard it would be, but there were other men
there who were going through the same thing. That seemed to strike a chord,
sort of if other men are doing it, I can do it too. It took quite a while to get
him settled in, but after he met his roommate and saw that he had everything
he was used to having, he settled down. I couldn't say the same for me. I kept
thinking of the baby elephant I had seen on *Nova* or some program, I don't
remember. All I recalled was the screaming little baby elephant that had been
taken from the herd to be trained for work by natives. He was chained to a
tree and prodded and poked at constantly to make him submit to his trainers.
Dad was like that when I left him, tears silently rolling down his cheeks,
mentally straining against the bonds of old age and that new unfamiliar place I
had taken him into. I cried myself sick when I got home.

OCTOBER 30

Dad had to be moved to nursing home care. He's really upset now. I gave him the bright colored log cabin quilt I made for his bed and we moved his bed from home to the room for him. When I gave it to him I told him that I loved him. He looked at me directly in the eyes and said astonishingly clearly, "I know, but it's not enough, is it." Strokes are very mysterious. This man who could not say what he meant to voice his daily needs, was able to give voice to his heart in that moment of deepest sadness. I felt crushed that I truly had given my best, and that it had not been enough. But I did stay with him, while his sons couldn't handle the emotional hurt his inability to converse with them brought. They didn't know that his heart was still the same.

NOVEMBER 12

I have been keeping in touch with my cousins from home. They call me if there are problems with Dad. I get down there as often as possible to stay for a few weeks. Troubles with medications given without my knowledge. Haldol?!! Made him a drooling idiot! That was my first battle. Zyprexa was the next. Atavan given in low doses is IT. Mercedes, my granddaughter, goes to visit him almost every day and takes him out in his wheelchair whenever it's warm enough. Nieces go often as well. Seems that now he's in a nursing home it makes it easier for them to go see him.

.

JUNE 23, 2001

Dad died in our arms last night at 10:30. I'm glad the rest of the family had gone and that Gene and I were the only ones left with him to soothe him. He was so afraid of dying. Gene said to him, "Just remember riding your horse beside the Snake River and feel the breeze blowing." Just ride on home with that wind. It helped him, soothed him into his next life.

JUNE 30

Took my camera out to photograph the morning glories by the back deck. Looking directly into the incredibly light-filled heart of the blossoms, I suddenly recalled looking into my babies' eyes and wondering at the perceived mystery there. I believe life gradually replaces some recollection of where we came from. I'd like to think that death will be a glorious remembering, an opening into sunlight for a spirit as fragile and evanescent as a blue morning glory blossom and as quiet and beautiful as their opening with the first rays of sunlight on a new day. ♣

2,000

A Portrait Journal

I've written diaries and journals since I was young; intermittent, sometimes passionate and required for sanity. Years later, they seem fresh and sometimes embarrassingly honest. Or, they remind me of things I intended to do, that never got done.

I wrote this journal as my mother painted my portrait during her final battle with breast cancer. We were both doing the one thing most important to us at the time, and we were doing it together. Although I attempted to expand it into a longer story, or reduce it to a poem, this is the version that lives.

Janice Wilson Stridick

TUESDAY, APRIL 25

We're in the room Mom calls the orangery, a sun porch she's claimed as her studio. We threw out all the spent tulips, salvaging the colored flags of those whose blooms had simply curled. Rearranging books, tables, and flowers with Mom reminds me of working with my husband Paul on our house. Both of these dear people – my closest friends – are artists in the truest sense. Visual truth, a sort of perfection, drives them. I have a sense of what's "right" and "wrong" in design, but Mom and Paul seek "truth."

She'd wanted more red, so I moved the crimson Emperor Tulip to the front. The room is pungent with tulips, daffodils, hyacinth, and generous boughs of dogwood. Mom has kept her winter flowers alive, too, so Christmas cactus and cyclamen ring the room on high glass shelves, determined not to cede the stage to their transient cousins.

Yesterday, she could barely walk or talk. I drove her to the hospital for a procedure in which they drained fluid from her lungs. While there, I learned to maneuver her canister of oxygen and the wheelchair she often depends upon.

Today I'm the stationery one, the subject. As Mom works, applying the pigment, she wants to capture the flowers before they wilt. She tells me that the green underpainting makes a complexion nice – you apply it under the peach and pink of flesh tones, she says. I think I'll try that when I'm applying make-up, say I. Not so fast, says she.

In the act of painting, Mom's strength and focus have returned. She stands at the canvas applying great swaths of pigment, defining her composition with shading and suggested nuance to be detailed later.

Her arms have a life of their own now; her eye commands them. She leans forward and back freely, heedless of her body's recent rebellions. It's hard to imagine her as she was yesterday, when she could barely sit in my car.

As I pose, I feel like part of a still life. I'm writing on a small notebook propped by a Pierre Deux pillow on my lap. The firm cotton paisley features gold and deep blue figures on a rich, red background. Bamboo towers behind me.

I'd love to curl up under Mom's mohair throw. I've been running, running, running and now – stopped – I just want to fold. Drowsily, as through a scrim, I hear birds singing, maybe chirping, but it sounds like a video recorder in rewind. I ask if Dad's rewinding anything. Mom says no.

THURSDAY, APRIL 27

The weather has been cool, gray and damp. I'm lulled by the white noise of Mom's portable heater, punctuated by the sound of her brush as it strikes the palette or the sides of her oilcan. Toothy sounds of bristle on canvas reassure me as she applies the paint.

She steals looks as her brush moves across the canvas. She leans back to view the composition and then picks up a small hand mirror and turns to view me, and her work, in reflection.

When the last glob of green squeezes onto her palette, she worries about running out; it's the basis of her underpainting, "Terre Verte."

As she paints, she whispers. "Yeah, that's the way the chair works. Now. How do the legs work? Way up there. Now hold onto that!" She commands me to maintain my pen on paper. "We've got the legs, and now we're working on hands."

Shortly after I settled myself into position, the crimson tulip made a dramatic exit. First, it folded in upon itself, then dropped a bit lower, then the petals burst off the stamen and littered my lap, the edge of the chair and the floor. As the weight of the petals fell, the stamen rose up, glistening and bare. The smell of tulip pollen drenched the air.

Mom paints as if nothing has changed. She has a harder time getting up and moving away from the canvas, but her focus and her animated approach haven't changed. She moves her upper body almost constantly. Her torso leans into the canvas, and then away, she angles in to view it differently. She twists to dip her brush into the oil, the color, to canvas – and back to her tin cup of turps to clean the pigment off and begin again.

Years ago, when she first started painting, she said she worked in oil because it was easier – she could fix it. She recalled her difficulty regarding the use of color.

"I would add something and be surprised at how out of balance it suddenly made my canvas." She said, "I didn't know how to anticipate the overall effect of changing just one small aspect of a painting."

The unforgiving medium of watercolor forced her to work fast and finish paintings. Today, as she approaches this life-sized portrait, she revels in the malleability of oil. I sense that she appreciates my malleability, also, and I hold still.

MONDAY, MAY 1

For our third sitting, the weather has finally decided to comply; it feels like spring. The sun is out and the forecast promises a kiss of 73-degree temperatures this afternoon.

Mom whispers to herself and moves her brush from color to canvas. She comes upon a rock-hard tube of paint, lights a match and holds it to the cap until the neck turns black and the match is charred – then she twists the cap off with a towel and squeezes pigment onto her palette. Today I can't write; I just want to watch. I suppose it's the effect of sunlight. I put down my pen and enjoy the flow of her energy all around me. She's unstoppable.

MAY 25

It's been three weeks since I posed for this hungry canvas. Things have changed. Only last week, I regretted the size and scope of the project: I feared it would end abruptly, unfinished. And I would find it impossible to view, knowing how important it has been to Mom to capture my image on canvas, and how reluctant I've been to sit still and subject us both to the disappointment of her illness, and her harsh judgment of her own work. I've avoided this place, but now as Mom's mortality plays across our family's stage, I must take the time to be with her and let her try to make this painting.

Perhaps the sentence is not so final. She's rallied once again to the canvas. Her surety with paint and brush is immutable. The bewilderment I've witnessed as she's suffered through an endless parade of chemical cures has no place in her studio. Here, she reigns. She knows exactly what to do.

So, of the past three weeks, what to tell? The breathing, which had become such a problem that she was constantly on high levels of oxygen, is no longer a problem. On May 8th she had surgery, an operation called a "pleurodisis"– where both of her lungs were drained. The four days she spent in the hospital almost killed her; to the surgeon and most of the nurses she was a dead woman.

Afterward, my sister Kate took her into Philadelphia to receive a rescue level of intravenous nutrition and oxygen. It was a heroic effort, and it worked. I had to be in a client meeting in Trenton, and when I returned, Mom was going without portable oxygen for the first time in six weeks. Then she started crabbing about the condition of her refrigerator, and bossing me around.

Since that day, she's had daily oxygen therapy, we've involved hospice care, and she's stabilized. She has no strength in her legs, but she can paint and cook and write letters. She and Dad are adjusting to a completely different pattern.

AUGUST 1, FIRST SITTING SINCE JUNE

Today when I arrived, I poured a glass of water for her and helped to set up her oil paints. The first tube of white undercoating was stuck and wouldn't budge, so I opened a newer one. It, however, had not been fully sealed and a plug of the pigment had solidified. Mom went after it with a matchstick, punching it back into the tube like a stubborn cork in a bottle of cheap wine.

One of the most valuable aspects of her art is the zone she enters while painting. There's no competition – no proving – unlike her bridge matches with Dad, or the battle with cancer, or even her feelings about maintaining cleanliness and order in her kitchen.

She just thanked me for pushing her to do this, and I'm grateful she feels that way. I asked, "Do you mean the portrait in general, or today's sitting?" She said, "Both, but I was thinking of today's sitting." She's forgotten that it was her idea to do the portrait.

As we viewed her progress a few minutes ago, she remembered feeling sad when the dogwoods lost their petals this spring. She thought they were her last ones. Today she thinks differently.

SUNDAY, AUGUST 27

Our competing schedules and Mom's failing health have made it almost impossible to find time to finish the portrait. In fact, when I called this morning to confirm our plan, she got irritated with me for asking her to block out time – she had just blocked out two and a half days for my sister Deb and she was tired of such efforts.

Also, as we began this session, she had a hard time coaching me into position. Apparently, her sight is failing. I offered to move the easel and paints up closer, but that would spoil the perspective, she said.

So, after all the challenges, she paints from her wheelchair and I hold my position, tracking the course of this, our presumably final mother-daughter collaboration.

Her painting commands attention. Now, as she mixes colors and fine-tunes the portrait, she's intensely focused. The wheelchair works well – allowing her to pull back and view the painting – then pull up close and apply brush strokes to the areas in question.

By the end of the session, she agrees to exhibit the canvas in her annual fall show in Cape May. It will be unsigned, a *'work in progress'* not for sale. She titles it *"Portrait of Jan."*

APRIL 30, 2001, "FIXING" THE PORTRAIT OF JAN

We had a lot of wrangling to get started – I had to get the easel and oil paints ready, find the little green milk stool for my feet, play with the trajectory of the light on my knee and adjust the window shade. But now we have, apparently, recreated the exact angle of my legs, the folds of my skirt, and Mom is satisfied that she can go ahead and perfect the painting.

She claimed she had "fifteen things to do" to correct the portrait. Although she said she'd done most of the fixes, I could see no difference.

At the end of our session, at my urging, she paints her initials in the bottom left corner. The white faces of the dogwood bear witness. ☙

2000

The Sky is Green

My husband and I immigrated to the U.S. from Iran in 2000. I promised myself I would keep a journal of my new life; a promise – regrettably – I never kept, at least the way I wanted.

Going through a revolution and eight years of war during my childhood and school years, I had many challenges. And then, as an Iranian living in the U.S. especially after 9/11 – with a deep emotional tie to my country – I faced even more challenges; one war after another, more death, blood, fear and darkness . . .

A young journalist in my mid-twenties and a young physician in his early thirties, my husband and I left our homeland and family and friends, not for "wealth," nor for a "better life;" not for "freedom" nor for "opportunities;" perhaps for all of the above? It is, however, fair to say we immigrated to explore . . . we are still exploring . . . aren't we all?

Our journey started in Austin, TX, where we lived for three months with my husband's cousin – who was and still is his best friend – and his wonderful wife. Many cities and states later, we finally settled in Baltimore, MD.

This entry was the first that I wrote after we immigrated. I have struggled to translate it without losing the original feeling, but of course, that is impossible.

Pantea A. Tofangchi

می گویم بیا و مثلا از جدایی! دیگر نباشیم . جدایی می دانی چیش خوب است ؟

اینش خوب است که تو از کسی یا از چیزی جدای شوی که به آن وابستگی

داشته ای! و این معنی خوب است که تو وابسته و عاشق باشی چون

آنوقت تعبدی شوی ! آنهم به چیزی که مقدس ترین بویه :

دنیاست : دوست داشتن ! بی آنوقت برای حفظ آن تلاش

خواهی کرد! این عالی نیست؟ دوست آنم که نگذشت مقدست تو را

یاد چی خدا هم ننداخت !

سنی محبت آسمانی دارد! نعمتی که آسمانی کرده است . ستاره ها آیام

آسمان پر از ستاره روست ! جالب ترازهمه اینکه من ستاره ها کدازهم

آسمان اول هم می بینی ؟! من که هنوز نداده به بازگشت نگذاشته ام که

به مدد رنگ آبی تعبّر دهم .

22/BAHMAN/1379 FEBRUARY 10, 2000

Whenever I feel like writing there is no pen and paper to be found and whenever there is, I don't feel like writing. And now that I want to write, I just have to write with this old yellow fountain pen, which is not working properly. The last time I used this fountain pen must have been to write an article in the *Zan Newspaper* back in Iran.

I knew there would be times when I would miss even the lousy and dirty street cats of Tehran. Twenty something days have passed and I don't even let myself think about my nostalgia, as it makes me too emotional; I might fly back home . . .

Austin is filled with violas and bluebonnets. So I can live here happily, although the sky seems a little bit low. It's as if I could reach the sky even though the feathery clouds are unreachable. There was a girl in a *Jack and the Beanstalk* cartoon who could make heart-shaped clouds from the clouds she was walking on. I wish I were she. What if I could fly or if I could travel in time. So far I have never seen a rainbow here. People in Austin applaud when the sun is setting. Why doesn't everybody celebrate sunset? Why are most people sad around dusk?

We are fine – I forgot to mention – except for little things: I wish I knew how to weave a rug, I wish I were a carpenter. And I haven't read a single Hafiz poem since I immigrated to the U.S. Nevertheless, I am the only one who knows all the secrets in Shahriar's innocent, unrivaled eyes. I wish I could foresee our future. What if some years from now I am still dreaming about the same wishes? What if there is no pomegranate tree or narcissus in our garden. I have a short story that I want to write the screenplay for.

I don't want this white paper to know all my silly wishes though.

Let's never be sad about being apart from home and family. Even if it causes you pain, it's so wonderful to be attached and dependent and involved and in love. Loyal to the grandest of all: caring! Therefore for keeping it you will strive!

And then wheat, which is also golden, will remind you of whom?

Wheat is of no use to me. The wheat fields have nothing to say to me. And that is sad. But you have hair that is the color of gold. Think how wonderful that will be when you have tamed me! The grain, which is also golden, will bring me back the thought of you. And I shall love to listen to the wind in the wheat. THE LITTLE PRINCE

Such a peculiar sky! I am talking about the stars. The sky is filled with the stars. Remarkable as it is, they are the same stars I used to watch in Iran?!

I am so lonesome here.
And every instrument I see sounds awful.
Let's pack provisions,
and step on a no return path;
see if the sky of "everywhere" is the same color? M. OMID FROM THE POEM CHAVOSHI, 1956

I haven't stepped on a no return path, why am I commenting on the color of the sky then? You know what though, I will decide on the sky's color: It should be Green! ❧

2001

My Breast Cancer Journey

I have been keeping a journal since the age of 10. Over the years, my journal has been my friend and confidant to help me through difficult times. I strongly believe in the powerful healing qualities of the written word.

Today, I teach journaling to breast cancer survivors and high-risk teens. During my breast cancer journey, writing became my lifeline and a way to give voice to my deepest feelings.

The following is an excerpt from my memoir/self-help book, *Healing With Words: A Writer's Breast Cancer Journey,* forthcoming in 2010.

http://www.dianaraab.com.

Diana M. Raab

AUGUST 22, ONE DAY POST-OP

I wake up in the Intensive Care Unit (ICU) today and Simon sits beside me holding my hand. One part of me wants to look down at the hospital gown covering this corset-like gauze bandage around my chest. Yet another part of me is scared out of my mind. The nurse helps me to the bathroom and I avoid the mirror as if it holds the most dreaded secret. I want to rip it off the bathroom wall. I never want to see myself naked. While walking back to bed, I look over at Simon and begin sobbing with no respite. I know in my heart that one day soon I will have to look at my chest. My hope is that my plastic surgeon will make all the necessary explanations. I am happy that the surgery is behind me, but now I must begin preparing to walk down an even more arduous road. I must get used to the new me.

AUGUST 23

Today my mood oscillates back and forth. One moment I want to touch my newly-created breast and the next minute I never want to see it. I am pleased that the reconstruction was done immediately following the mastectomy. After breakfast, I pulled the nurse's cord to help me sit up. I am terribly sore from being in one position. By the time she arrives moments later, I have already changed my mind. I put my hand over my right breast and feel nothing. I do the same on the left. I can only feel the slight pressure of my hand. How will I ever get used to having no sensations. My right nipple had always been more sensitive and easily stimulated than my left, but now there is a sense of nothingness, numbness, a void.

Today the nurse removed the bandage around my chest. I looked the other way while crying into my pillow. I felt nothing. My plastic surgeon said some sensations might eventually return, but never again could I become sexually aroused on my right side. So, I have two breasts, but really only one. My sensations have been severed forever. Never again would I experience that sublime tingling when Simon runs his fingers over my rather large nipple – never again on that side. Never could I experience the joy and tingles from let-down reflex when my babies sucked for the first time. I loved that sensation which permeated my soul and brought me such joy.

AUGUST 27

The books I have read, and my nursing experience warned me that depression is common following many surgeries, particularly breast surgery, because of the huge psychological component of losing a breast. I should be optimistic because my breast surgeon says that the cancer has been removed. He says I am lucky that it did not spread into my lymph nodes. Yes, this is a true blessing, but there are moments when this is not enough to console me. My father taught me to look at the glass half full and not half empty. I'm trying. Really trying. But, this entire event has been surreal. My defenses are stripped. I have no strength left in my body except for the weeping. Tears flow like an endless river. They pour out without warning and dry up without notice.

AUGUST 28

I look around me and see all the technology. I think of my husband, an engineer, and how people like himself have made mine and so many others' survival possible. He is a fixer. On so many other occasions he wants to quickly make everything better for me. His smile and touch are so healing. He has so much power, but he cannot bring my breast back to me. He says he wishes he had a magical wand to make me feel better. I tell him that the wand was discarded the day it brought him into my life. One person cannot be bestowed with any more luck than me. He implores me to think positively.

Sometimes life is not so simple. I don't want to say this to him because he tries so hard to soothe me. It's still early in my post-operative period, but I already feel physically and emotionally changed and drained. In some ways it is easier being far from home. My predicament somehow seems clearer and my mind less distracted by familiar surroundings.

SEPTEMBER 3

Today I am nearly two weeks post-op. I do not feel any better emotionally than the day they rolled me out of the cold and sterile operating room. My emotional strength is barely returning. I still get teary-eyed for no obvious reason. This morning, the nurses bathed me. They helped me to the chair where I tried reading a magazine, but my mind wandered. Everything makes me cry, even glancing at the latest hairstyles in the magazine. I feel trapped inside this body that I don't know anymore.

SEPTEMBER 4

Today I will go visit my plastic surgeon. It seems as if the past couple of weeks have been surreal. A thick cloud suspends over me. How did I get here? I was diligent about my annual mammograms and check-ups. On the first day of my menstrual cycle I diligently did breast self-exams in the shower. There is no cancer in my family. Why am I lying here all mutilated?

I have never thought much about cancer, but one thing I know is that if cancer is in your body, you better get it out quickly.

Having had reconstructive surgery at the same time as my mastectomy has put my mind at ease. Even though I have refrained from looking at myself naked in the mirror, there was a sense of relief to waking up with a mound on my right side, even if it was not my own breast, but just a sack of saline water.

SEPTEMBER 6

I'm trying to take the position that cancer is no longer lurking inside of me. I did have cancer, but it is now all gone. All of it.

I am so afraid that the cancer will come back. I cry about losing the breast and also about having to lose my other one. Crying comes so easily. Sometimes the tears last a few minutes, other times an hour. It all depends.

2001

Flight Journal September 11, 2001

Recently I've been blaming age for failing memory, but then realize that, perhaps, I might not be as decrepit as I think. Failing memory could result from not keeping a journal.

I first started keeping one in the form of a diary when I was 13 after reading Anne Frank's *The Diary of a Young Girl* . Over the years, I've kept it up sporadically, although always when I travel. Travel is so transitory. I want it to last, to make it permanent.

When I don't keep a journal, life rushes by like the view from a train window, events smudge, become grainy. But when I do, I find myself focusing on what's going on around me. Once something is in writing, I tell myself, it's less likely to disappear. And, on another level, I can't help believing that once I've put it in writing, I'm less likely to disappear.

Diana Anhalt

SEPTEMBER 11
ON DELTA FLIGHT 119 PARIS-NEW YORK. AROUND 1:00 P.M.

Just a few hours ago our pilot announced, "Air space over the United States has been closed to air traffic due to a terrorist act. Our plane has been diverted to St. John's, Newfoundland. I will give you more information, as it is forthcoming."

I'd been reading Peter Canby's brilliant book, *The Heart of the Sky,* about his travels among the Maya, and I had just reached the line: "At 3:30 in the afternoon the wheels fell off my progress toward Nebaj." Well, at that very moment, the wheels fell off our progress to New York. My first reaction was disbelief. "Estos gringos siempre exageran," I scoffed. ("These gringos always overreact.") Mauricio, my Mexican husband, agreed. But I know my reaction is mere bravado. For once in my life I've actually tasted fear. (It tastes bitter, like burnt coffee.)

Shortly before 11 a.m. our plane landed in St. John's. We can move about freely, the back door has been opened, and they're now projecting *Moulin Rouge.* (No one's watching.) Awhile ago I headed toward the back of the plane. (We're flying Business Class.) Bits of information are leaking in via cellular phone, and a passenger in possession of a radio turned up the volume. Some 30 passengers hovered in the aisles or leaned over seat backs straining to hear: "The World Trade Center is gone." "Rogue planes loaded with explosives have disappeared." "A plane flying off course in Pennsylvania has been shot down." "Three hundred fire fighters are dead." Rumors fly fast and furious. (Nothing else does.) We are stuck in a plane and parked on a runway with nowhere to go. Stranded.

Beyond the window of our cabin soldiers are deployed in the area just beyond our plane. I watch as passengers of a United Airlines jet disembark and are directed to a patch of grass at the far end of the field. (Rumor has it they've received a bomb threat.)

SEPTEMBER 12, 9:30 A.M.
THE HMCS CABOT COAST GUARD INSTALLATION

So much to write about, but as it turns out we'll have plenty of time, two or three days at least. I'm trying to reconstruct events while they're still fresh in my mind.

Yesterday, as night fell, the headlights of police cars, ambulances and fire engines illuminated the field. At about 11p.m. a truck towing the disembarkation stairs approached our plane. (The airport, accustomed to receiving no more than one or two international flights daily, has only one of these and it took over eight hours to evacuate the 27 planes of some estimated 4,200 passengers and 400 in crew.) Before we were allowed to vacate the plane, paramedics, accompanied by soldiers, carried two people requiring medical attention off our plane.

Although we were allowed no luggage, only passports and boarding passes, the women were permitted their handbags. I took eyeglasses, currency, a book, a notebook and ballpoint pen, lipstick, foundation and eye pencil. Then my Girl Scout survival skills kicked in. I included socks, toothpaste and toothbrushes, drinking water and peanuts. (As it's turned out the last thing we need is food.)

Thus, some 19 hours after having left Paris, at approximately 11:30 p.m.

Newfoundland time, which for some reason is one and a half hours later than Eastern Standard Time, we left the plane, diverted to this small Canadian city, home to some 130,000 people.

Mauricio carried blankets and pillows, I paper bags with sandwiches and energy bars, handed out by volunteers. (I rapidly wolfed down a tuna sandwich. We'd had nothing much since morning. I think it's the best sandwich I've ever tasted.) How rapidly we'd traveled from being global travelers to becoming "refugees." For a moment I thought of my grandmother and that long line of immigrants I am descended from.

Making our way across the tarmac toward the terminal I felt a sense of detachment. All eyes were on us. (Ordinarily I go through life observing, not being observed.) Where had I seen this scene before? Crowds moving through the dark carrying blankets and food? A Spielberg film? *On the Beach*?

As we passed through a security cordon, a policeman quipped, "Last summer weather we'll see this fall. 78-degrees today. In winter the snow rises higher than the telephone poles."

"Shut up, Howie," said his companion. "We want these folks to come back again, as tourists."

SEPTEMBER 12, 5:30 P.M.

We left the airport on buses and proceeded to the processing center, the Mile One Hockey Stadium, probably the largest facility in town, where the press and assorted relief workers – the Salvation Army, St. John's Ambulance and the Red Cross, along with hordes of volunteers – received us. Loud speakers barked out instructions in some fifteen languages. (They were trying to recruit a Russian translator.) One young man, his hair in a ponytail, stood off to one side, and signed instructions for the hearing impaired. Volunteers dispensed coffee, soap, toothbrushes and toothpaste. Doctors, nurses, social workers, counselors and pharmacists were available to assist those who required medical or psychological assistance.

Initially, we were registered, sorted out by flight number and seated in a vast arena where we witnessed the devastation of the World Trade Center beamed onto the stadium's scoreboard. I don't think anything can prepare you for this kind of destruction – particularly when it entails a national landmark. Also targeted: the Pentagon. One plane crashed into a field when passengers tried to stop terrorists.

Telephone banks had been installed to permit free long-distance dialing anywhere worldwide. We were able to get through to both kids. (Laura told us that without the World Trade Center the view from her balcony has changed drastically.)

We were fortunate. While many passengers were farmed out to schools, churches, the convention center and private homes, we were sent to the HMCS Cabot Coast Guard installation, where we were greeted by its Commanding Officer, Margaret Morris, and herded into the main lounge. All the television sets aired reports of the debacle. (And for the first time we were able to assemble bits and pieces of info we'd picked up in the course of the day.)

Since private rooms are scarce, we were asked to accept communal accommodations and were assigned two spaces alongside the window of the 14-bed dormitory. We have been given toilet supplies – soap, deodorant, shampoo, etc. but no towels – not yet. We are lucky to have a bed – well, make that a cot – to call our own.

We spent an uneasy night. Whenever I shifted position the cot creaked. If I pulled up the blanket to protect my neck, my feet froze. Nor am I used to sleeping entirely clothed – and we are all charged up by past events and the uncertainty of the coming days. I dozed briefly but both Mauricio and I were up by 6 a.m. After showering and drying myself off with paper towels I dressed in yesterday's clothes and returned to Dorm E. I spotted a man in briefs and undershirt sauntering down the hall. On our way to breakfast we passed the gymnasium and caught sight of hundreds of people bedded down, one alongside the other, in sleeping bags. (We are indeed lucky.)

Throughout breakfast we joked at the contrast between our meals in Paris and our simple – but hearty – buffet breakfast. Feeling the need for exercise, Mauricio and I walked toward town, but were immediately identified as "stranded passengers" and were given a lift by a friendly local. Everyone is eager for news of us. We too are news, and Canada is, of course, an integral part of the relief effort. All of the papers and broadcasts include "stranded passenger" stories.

St. John's, partially picturesque, partially seaside seedy, is dotted with clapboard houses with shuttered windows and resembles a New England fishing town. The main street is lined with small stores, tourist agencies, coffee shops and restaurants.

I purchased a cherry red sweater and underwear, Mauricio a fresh shirt and socks. We spend our time here reading the papers and watching the news, which worsens as death tolls rise.

Have been particularly struck by some of those we've come in contact with: a French-speaking grandmother with two young children; a Christian zealot who prays all the time and was horrified when she asked my religion and I told her I didn't have one; Marissa Berenson, a model and one-time film star with her arrogant French husband. (Her sister was killed in one of the planes that went down with the terrorists); some lovely French, American and Asian honeymoon couples; a grass hockey coach; three Senegalese diplomats and a former back stroke swimming champ; a violinist.

SEPTEMBER 13, 5:30 P.M.

We've been watching TV and munching on potato chips and popcorn. A Belgian woman tells me she's unable to sleep on the floor of the gymnasium so she waits until the lounge is deserted and then spreads her sleeping bag out on a sofa. (She's not alone.)

Tonight the view is particularly beautiful: Light from streetlamps across the inlet and from surrounding homes and buildings dapples the wet pavement, and mist rises from the water. The Belgian woman said, "That mist is particularly appropriate – it suits my mood." (I guess we're all feeling a little gloomy.)

This morning the view from the dormitory window of harbor and shore, small craft, the occasional house and the friendly black stray who has made the base his home, has changed overnight. A large white ship has moored on the opposite shore.

We'd been awoken by the blast of loud speakers at 6 a.m. "Will all Sabena personnel please proceed to the main desk?" and for a minute hope, at half-mast, for the past two days rose in my chest – not for long. In the bathroom speculation ran rampant. Most agreed the plane was returning to Belgium because foreign airlines are being directed back to their place of origin. So, rather than allow ourselves to be swayed by winds of optimism, Mauricio and

I went to the mall to buy tomorrow's underwear.

At a brief meeting, held by Delta this afternoon, we heard that the Sabena flight took off at around 3 p.m. During the meeting the cordiality and good will which has marked our stay and sustained us over the past three days collapsed. Two flight attendants and a pilot attempted to explain that we'll be leaving tomorrow and tried to outline some sort of procedure. Flying into New York at this time is untenable, so we will be moved to an open airport, probably Cincinnati. But a handful of passengers, claiming that TV reports indicated otherwise, flew into a rage and insisted on establishing their own conditions. Pandemonium ensued.

We've learned via the local paper, delivered to us daily, that the Senegalese diplomats we'd spoken to at breakfast yesterday refused to return to Europe and requested diplomatic asylum.

SEPTEMBER 14, 10:30 P.M.

On the morning of Friday 14, I crawled into Mauricio's cot and we giggled at Myrna and George, our early risers, who groped their way through the dark, dropped coins, bumped into cots, and fumbled through shopping bags – they had accumulated enough merchandise to stock a store. Then from the sound system: "Will all passengers on Delta Flight #119 please prepare for departure? We will board buses at 8:30 a.m." Some of our bunkmates started to cheer. We made a beeline for the bathrooms.

The information nerve center at Cabot Coast Guard base is the ladies room. Rumors fly – again: One woman told us she found a man sleeping in her bed; someone said that the large ship is part of the *Titanic* exploration project, and the grandmother traveling with two young children said she'd heard her plane was unlikely to leave for two more days. (She burst into tears when I said goodbye.)

After a breakfast of canned baked beans – for me one of the highlights of the experience – and an affectionate farewell from those who have remained behind, we were bused to the Mile One Stadium, and processed. Then we waited until 11 a.m. After being transported to the airport, we waited again for about an hour – until the previous plane had left. We passed through rigid security and several metal detectors, claimed our in-cabin possessions, identified and opened all baggage, had our passports checked against our tickets, boarded the plane and had our passports checked again. It's about 3:30 New York time – and we're on our way to Cincinnati, the second U.S. flight out of Saint John's. We've been lucky. It's rumored that from there we may be bused to N.Y. ♣

2003

Iraqi Freedom War Board

I started writing a journal at age thirteen after I read Anne Frank's *The Diary of a Young Girl* and discovered a diary could be about more than schoolyard gossip. It could be about feelings and wonder. It could record dreams and observations from which poetry could evolve. It is my therapy through difficult emotional times. Where I hoard experiences I don't want to lose. When I "come in here" to write in my journal, I am in a place that is all my own.

Simki Ghebremichael

APRIL 5

Friday we racked up a victory for our side. I've been so depressed at work – sublimating my outrage, my dissent to the overall pro-occupation stance of my colleagues. They put up an "Iraqi Freedom War Board" pinning up mostly anti-French cartoons and protestor-bashing editorials. One cartoon showed the Statue of Liberty with a bare ass.

When they put up a conversation between a Native American, a cowboy and a Muslim, that ended with the cowboy declaring the Muslims were many in number because "we hadn't played cowboys and Muslims yet," I knew I had grounds to protest the blatant racism. And besides, aren't we supposed to be liberating the Muslims? Did these people care about Iraqi children before George Bush told them to?

My feet marched me into the office of the Human Relations Manager, a congenial, freckle-faced man who had lectured us on diversity and harassment in the workforce. He had encouraged us to come to him if we encountered a problem. I didn't know that he was African-American until I saw the photos of his family and the art on his wall. I never saw a white executive who had a picture by the artist, Jacob Lawrence, and a wife and daughter whose skin was the color of creamy caramel.

I was very nervous. The Manager was ready to walk back with me to my department, but I said, "No, I'm just informing you." When he stopped by the next morning, Mike overheard him telling Ellen that he came "to check the decorum of the board" because someone had been offended by it. Mike and Bruce immediately called me over for a meeting of the three Team Leads. "Someone has gone to HR saying they were offended by the messages on the board."

"That would be me," I owned up.

Bruce expressed disappointment that I hadn't brought it up to him and Mike first so we could handle it internally. I said I felt insecure because I didn't know who was in charge of the board. I had already penciled in a rebuttal to one of them. The one about the only land we've ever taken in our many foreign wars was the ground our soldiers were buried in. I wrote: "It's about resources, not land." Peter [my husband] says I should have written: "Texas. California."

Mike and Bruce looked at the board with new eyes and decided most of it was offensive and we should call a meeting to say it was unacceptable. We all trooped down to HR to let the Manager know our solution to the problem. He gave us some words to use, "decorum" being his favorite.

At the meeting, Bruce said that we were going to take down the offensive materials. It was alright to have a Support the Troops board but the tone at present was too negative. Phil asked who had been offended. Bruce and Mike said it wasn't relevant, Bruce said if you have to think for a moment about whether something is acceptable, it probably isn't, and you shouldn't put it up. But if something lacking in decorum goes up, the Team Leads will take it down.

Shelly piped up in her totally off the charts bombastic way about whether the Thought Police would be preventing us from putting things up in our own cubicles. Mike said, "No, that is your own space." Some seemed discomfited that one offended person should ruin it for the others. I repeated what the HR Manager had said to us, that it only takes one to be offended and then it's not appropriate. LaVonne, who has been taking human resource classes; corroborated that. Shelly said things like, "Well, if they don't like it, they can just walk on by, not look at the board." LaVonne said, "You have to look at it once to read it."

Then they wondered how the Team Leads were going to be able to decide what was appropriate. They didn't like the idea of anyone deciding for them. There was hardly any discussion on this point. Bruce just said, "Well, unless we get to be the arbiters, the wall is coming down." And so they voted for no wall. I'm guessing some just wanted to use the wall to vent and be negative. They didn't really want to support the troops.

Shelly went on a tirade against the poor female POW from West Virginia who Shelly thought was getting entirely too much publicity and probably hadn't even been shot through with bullets and slapped around by her captors.

Others were just ready to see the wall come down. Lauren spoke for someone who was absent, "Scott didn't like any part of the wall." The episode brought out murmurings from other dissenters that heartened my spirits.

Hooray for our side. A good day. ♣

2004

G. W. Bush

I'm 73, and watching another actual war in living color from the comfort of my couch brought home again the horror and hopelessness of all those other endless wars. This journal entry just grew and grew. When will we ever learn?

Sally Pearson Congleton

NOVEMBER

The election has come and gone and George W. Bush won by about a 3% margin, and I have not been enthused enough to write about it. His "holiness" has convinced the people that homosexuality and abortion are moral issues but death by starvation and war are not.

Tonight we are totally destroying the city of Fallujah. To attack a country like Iraq, kill their people, ruin their infrastructure, and think they will vote to be a Democracy – like us? I don't think so! I have lived to be 70 years old but never thought I would live to see my country attack another nation for no reason.

Any war has its effect on all of us. This farm my husband and I own is said to be a Revolutionary War prize given to a particular soldier and handed down through the family until we were able to buy it at a public auction to settle the estate of the last heirs.

The stories I like to tell about my father's farm at Brassfield, Kentucky have their roots in the Civil War. The church we attend, Mt. Zion Christian Church, sat right in the middle of the Battle of Richmond and served as a field hospital for both the North and the South. The amputated limbs piled outside the windows didn't need labels.

Before the start of World War II, the United States government took the best farmland out of the heart of Madison County, Kentucky (14,000 acres) and built a huge ordnance depot on it. Many families were dislocated, they had no choice in the matter. Of course it brought new jobs to the area. It is now called the Bluegrass Army Depot and stores ammunition and poison gas. Old munitions were destroyed regularly, just across the road from us. The date for destroying the poison gas and the method to use are still being argued over.

When George Bush were looking for all those "weapons of mass destruction" I wanted to write and tell him where some of ours was hidden but he had ignored my letter, already sent, begging him not to start another war! ♣

2006

Obsessive Graphomania

I began my journal on May 6, 1977, shortly after graduating from the University of Michigan, writing in green cartridge-pen ink. I subsequently filled about 75 spiral notebooks, three feet of shelf space, writing on every line and on both front and back of every page, almost always using a cartridge-pen (though usually not green ink.)

On November 30, 2001 I switched to keeping my journal on my laptop computer. Since then I have created 24 MS-Word journal documents, each of roughly 100,000 words or more.

Is this obsessive graphomania sheer neurosis? What was I supposed to do with my life but failed to do because I was too busy writing in my journal?

Lee Warner Brooks

FRIDAY DECEMBER **8**

. . .

12H.

It sometimes seems that, unless I climb to the summit of the Everest of my abilities, I can't write really well.

And, of course, it's hard to breathe up there. Hard to survive.

I just spent almost an entire period just reading and grading one paper for one student – I think at least 40 minutes. That shows why it took so long for me to get thru the papers, especially this last set, Paper 4. I felt obligated to write comments and a note at the end that not only justifies the grade but explains, in some fashion, how to go about getting a better grade.

If my plan is indeed to try to become a successful 21st-century poet based on mastering and modernizing the sonnet form, then certain things follow:

> 1. I do need to become an expert in the form, at least in some sense and to some degree, by both reading sonnets from different eras and reading scholarly work that is relevant – that is, not just Vendler on WS's sonnets, but Fussell on meter and form, and so on.
>
> 2. I need to develop a better rationale for my project, a more precise notion of what a sonnet is and why I believe it is a perfect form for a 21st-century American poet to employ and why it suits me in particular to write in this form.

Both of those points raise a lot of issues. I've rebelled against the notion that I need to become an expert in anything, and yet it's obvious that people crave and expect expertise from writers – that is, not only wisdom, but expertise about something in particular. As a writer, you can to some degree pick the thing or things you want to claim expertise in, and you can direct questioners in such a way as to talk about what you know and avoid what you don't. But you need to have a set of talking points.

I saw that last summer at Frost Place. People wd ask me some very specific questions about whose writing I was modeling my writing after and what books guided my approach and so forth. I managed to handle those questions, but not as gracefully and forcefully as I'd have liked.

It is also a theory of mine that a lot of poets have gaping holes in their resumes and in their backgrounds. Many are in a sense autodidacts who've read deeply in a certain kind of stuff but are woefully deficient in other areas. And I think this is known – or at least intuited – and expected. But poets are still expected to be experts in something.

In my case, it cd be sonnets, but I'm far from being an expert in this now.

And it certainly is problematic that there are a lot of sonnets that I don't like. In that bookstore in New Hampshire, I picked up a nice paperback book stuffed full of Elizabethan sonnets by various writers – and put it back down. I knew I wdn't read it. Looking at it, I knew I didn't want to read it. I knew it wd be advantageous to have read it, but, things being the way they are, what are the chances I'd get to that point?

The point, I suppose, is that writing a good sonnet is hard, and it is not commonly done. Many people have attempted it. Many have fallen short. No one has been uniformly successful – even Shakespeare has some clinkers in there, some, for example, that are more clever than good, some that are valiant but failed experiments.

So it's fine for me to say that there are only a few sonneteers I admire, but I need to say that advisedly. If I'm going to reject whole centuries of writing out of hand, I'd better do some homework first, so I can defend my position, or at least not sound clueless in propounding it.

One concept I have is that the sonnet is perfect for this era, when everyone feels so pressed for time. Everyone has time to read a sonnet. You could put them on subway cars or buses. You could put them on road signs, but you'd have to put them one line at a time, like Burma-Shave signs. You cd read one while sitting at a traffic light or waiting for your computer to boot up.

People cd take two minutes a day and read one sonnet. It will fit easily into anyone's schedule.

16H.

Today worked well, I think. I went to each of the classrooms during class time and essentially did whatever was needed. Some students needed to ask questions or allay concerns, some needed to turn things in or get things turned back, some spent some time working on their papers, others simply needed to use that time for other things, and therefore did not stop by at all.

I like this concept of lightening up at the end, so students feel less pressure and have more time to wrap up their semester. I remember what a nightmare the end of the semester always seemed to be.

Had my appointment w/ Dr. Mertz today, and everything was fine – prostate unchanged, PSA about 1.7, which is right in my usual range, and today's urine sample was normal – no infection, no sugar imbalance, no blood.

Glad to have the prostate exam behind me, as it were, for another year.

Yesterday, caught a few minutes of one of those PBS shows of some know-it-all lecturer speaking in front of the usual absurdly warm-hearted and gullible audience. I never did catch his name; his theme in this segment was that we don't have "one true self," and that it's a mistake to spend our lives seeking that "true self." He said we all have many selves, and we shd not panic when asked to try a new one; we shd relax, and try for a "breakthrough" rather than a "breakdown." That was catchy, I thought.

I didn't entirely go for his message – I see my effort to be a lawyer as a perhaps overly open-minded effort to "break through" into a new self. In fact, I never found that new self; in fact, I did end in a breakdown.

OTOH, I recall reading that book about creative "breakthroughs" and how to achieve them; I still have it on my shelf – *Creative Breakthroughs: Tap the Power of Your Unconscious Mind,* by Jill Morris, PhD. I don't recall just when I read it, but I know that for a long time I've found myself recurring fairly often to this image of breaking through some confining obstruction – I believe it often looks, to my mind, somewhat like the "glass ceiling" journalists often talk about, the one that keeps women and minorities from rising to the highest levels in their professions. It's flat and horizontal and just over my head. And it seems to be impermeable.

When thinking of this ceiling, I have typically ended up privately bemoaning the indifference, ignorance, and injustice that keeps it there, and that prevents me – an unknown from nowhere – from breaking through it at any point. If only I knew someone, if only I cd get one of those gatekeepers to give my work a fair reading . . .

And so my moaning fades off into the night.

In one of those "thinking outside the box" moments today, while driving down I-94 to my urologist appointment, it struck me that I've been looking at this barrier from the wrong perspective – I've been setting myself up for breakdown, not breakthrough.

In fact, the seemingly impermeable barrier that divides me from success is not some tough, double-thick polymer created by the massive indifference of the world outside – appealing and plausible as that image is. The barrier really is a sort of cocoon that I have spun around myself. If I am trapped inside an eggshell, weakly striving to peck my way to freedom, it is an eggshell of my own making.

Now – does this clever rephrasing of the issue actually have any practical value? Does it allow me to alter my writing or submissions process in any way so as to make it more effective, or to change my life in some way so that I can reach goals that have heretofore eluded me?

Well, I don't know. But the idea arose from my thinking this morning about how I need to climb to the summit of Everest if I'm to have any hope of writing well. It does seem as tho, at this point, the few things I've published have been the tippy top of my achievement. Perhaps the truth is that my talent is so meager that only its extremest accomplishments will ever get noticed, and all the rest of what I do will pass deservedly unnoticed.

But if you look at what I do – I have, literally, millions of words that I've written during my adult life, over the past 30 years, at the cost of God-knows-how-many thousands of hours of scribbling and typing. But most of those words have landed in my Journal, where they are destined to be read by no one – most of them, not even read by me.

A great deal of thought has gone into those words, just as a great deal of thought is going into what I'm writing at this moment. I feel a great urgency to get these words down; I'm hopeful that this process of self-analysis and self-discovery will lead me at last into some better place.

And yet, and yet – look at what I'm doing. Other writers are using their writing time to write things that may get published. I'm using the great majority of my writing time to to write things that will never get published.

Surely this is a mistake. Surely this Journal is, in a sense, the cocoon that is swaddling me in confining thicknesses of some seemingly impermeable substance. It is my own introversion, my own fear of self-exposure, my own deep ambivalence, that I need to break through if I'm to have any hope of achieving my goal of being an author, rather than just a scribbler.

My habits, in short, are effective in calming my anxieties and panics, but very much counterproductive in terms of making the transition to being a published writer.

Not that I've failed completely. I still suspect that this bizarre obsession w/ Journalizing has in some ways made me the writer I've become. It has, at least, played a significant part in making my skills take shape. But I think I need to break out of this pattern, at least to some degree. I think I need to figure out a way to modify my habits, and slant my efforts more toward producing publishable work.

If the Journal is nothing but a security blanket, I might as well be dead – that's plenty secure – pain-free, anxiety-free.

But any plan needs to take reality into account, including, or especially, psychological reality. I do have anxieties; I do panic at times; I am fraught w/ ambivalence; it does take me a lot of time to recover from self-exposing experiences. Any plan that ignores these realities is liable to lead not only to failure, but to breakdown.

My attempt to be a lawyer tried to sail into the teeth of these psychological realities. My decision to become a writer was intended to sail w/ my own psychological winds filling my sails. I've got to take the next step, tho. ♣

2006

The Coal Company vs. The Family Cemetery

I started my journaling in response to the millennium and my 60th birthday.

I keep my journals online. Each year I adopt a different style or layout, and then I play with the content and format throughout the year, usually making only minor changes. At the end of the year, I print the pages and put them into a book. I sometimes take notes in a hard copy notebook and then expand them online.

I do not write in my journal daily. It works best for me to write weekly or several times a week. Most often my journal entries are sparked by something I have read or heard, or by changes in nature that I observe: birds, animals, plants.

Mary F. Whiteside

Small rural burying grounds dot the mountains and hollows of Appalachia (including West Virginia the home of my parents and grandparents), often in the same areas where coal companies continue their destructive practices of maintaintop removal mining. Greed drives people and businesses to such ruinous practices. Imagine ignoring something as sacred to rural communities and to society in general as cemeteries.

I wonder about the small family cemetery on the hill behind my mother's "home place" in Flaggy Meadow, WV. That old cemetery was located on the edge of a hill up behind the house, in a pasture used by my grand-father for his mules and cows. Surrounded by an old wire fence, protected by a few trees, the cemetery captivated me. I liked to go up there and sit among the stone markers, always wondering who the people were who were buried

Nell, my mother's favorite sister (the eldest sister, who had died in 1921 when my mother was 13) was buried there. Years later Nell was moved to the family plot in the Mannington, WV Cemetery. I was at grandpa's the day Nell Was to be moved. I was excited. I wanted to see inside the casket. I had all kinds of ideas about what would be there. But, when the mules pulled the wagon down all I saw was a big gray vault.

King Coal has been cheating the people of Appalachia since mining began. Now, as if ruining mountains weren't enough, coal companies are obliterating cemeteries. How can people hang on to their history and heritage when their land and their artifacts are wiped out?

Mary F. Whiteside

2006

One Year after My Divorce

Writing isn't a hobby for me. It's not just something I love to do. It is, quite simply, what keeps me alive. In some ways, it's how I know that I am alive. That's what I tell myself when I wonder why I write – all those hours of scratching pen on paper, scraping my heart to get to something I may never find, wish I'd never found, or was never ever there. It's a poorly planned, un-researched archaeological excavation. All I know is that my journals feed my poems and my stories – the ones that make it to print and those that don't, as surely as they feed me. And that I must eat to live.

Lalita Noronha

AUGUST 25
I. ONE YEAR AFTER MY DIVORCE

Summer's end. The days have gone – drowned in paint colors as delicious as champagne gold and dusky blue, copper pot. Colors like Comfort, evoking what the senses want, even though it goes on the wall – as if one could paint the heart in such colors.

A year after the papers were signed, you sealed your betrayal with wedding vows (Were they vows?) You flew to Las Vegas in the hollow of the night, telling no one, not even the children we made together, and flew to a new life with a new wife, twenty years younger, not much older than your daughter. We learn this in pieces, one by one, like strangers who talk about the weather in elevators, how the summer has gone, the days getting shorter, and all the children will return to school, as I will too – to the cadence and the rhythm of a newer reality, harsher perhaps, or maybe not, harsher, yes – cleaner than death, for in death one never knows where one goes, but divorce, and remarriage so soon after, is revealing – exposing what I should have known, knew in fact, but couldn't look betrayal and deception in the face– so dazzling is that coin, those two sides of a coin, beauty and youth on one face, the pocks of time on the other; it was all the difference between falling in and out of love.

II. THE WALL

You watch how the days have worn you down like the sandpaper.
You scrape the days, one hour at a time with coarse, then fine sandpaper,
smoothing out the dents you filled with putty, the nails where pictures hung,

trying not to inhale the dry wall worn down the way your spirit has been.

Smoothing, blowing the dust, sanding again, your hand on the brown piece, the coarseness aligned over the filled uneven dent. You want to get it right, smooth, smoother than it ever was, the grain perfectly aligned. When it is painted, champagne gold or comforting, should you use sage or copper pot, the colors that matter? What will scatter the light, soften the glare, deepen the grain? What will cover the cracks; the finest hairline cracks that no one will see existed there – not even you?

III. THE CHAIR RAIL

It can't be maple, even if it's ideal, matches the cabinets, highlights the grain. Chair rails aren't sold in maple, not at Lowes or Home Depot, or some lumber store. So I'll settle for yellow pine, twelve feet long, two and a half inches wide. That must be stained and polyurethaned, aligned to perfect size, the corner edges aligned, nailed with slender nails using a nail gun, the clean quick shots, none of this hammering and missing one's finger, driving it straight through wood and dry wall. It is secured now, well in place; it sections the wall, the top two thirds for what was – champagne – a honey gold. The bottom third for what will be copper pot, a brick red. But under both is dry wall, plastered, sanded, now painted, new, flawless, a room ready to be moved into, to start all over, except for those muted shadows on the wall that come alive at night, after the sun goes down here.

And rises on another. ♣

2006

Journal Keepings: Spring into Summer

I've been a journal keeper for 44 years. I'm the author of *One Journal's Life* (Impassio Press) and I co-founded the Life Writing Connection with LWC Director Olivia Dresher.

As Emerson addressed an "unknown friend" in his journals, I write to my journal as my "old compañero."

Audrey Borenstein

I am a receiver, and therefore have ESP of projections from anyone with a gift for "sending." Either that, or imagination and paranoia sometimes can combine to generate amazing stories with which one can entertain (if that is the word) oneself.

H. and I at the Vassar College exhibit "Grand Gestures: Celebrating Rembrandt" this 400th anniversary year of his birth – his prints, his art on paper, are from Vassar's permanent collection. H. brought me one of the hand-held magnifying glasses for visitors, and I put it to good use. Many (Christian) religious drawings, some Dutch landscapes . . . and drawings of beggars, burghers. And portraits – these I loved most of all. I could feel the wind in the trees; and the human-ness and drama of the moment of his creation of each work. Shadows and Rembrandtean light . . . his fascination with theatre, with "costumes". . . "I'm all out at the eyes!" I said to H. finally, and sank down on one of the benches. She came and sat down next to me. Side by side, we drew the afternoon into ourselves . . . Before leaving, we also visited the sculpture garden. Azaleas in profusion, of a red so exuberant, burning too deeply, as though it dreamed itself into being on this planet, from another world . . . On the way home, I told her about my old professor's blindness; she sang a song her mother used to sing. We talked about Christianity, Judaism, Islam – what they share, and what they do not share . . .

Nearly two weeks since I last communicated with you, old compañero. One grows ever more silent as one nears the shore – at least, this one does. Need I beg your pardon? One ought to write when the spirit moves one – and my spirit did not. I think these horrible times crush it – or very nearly do.

O, what this country has become; my heart is sick with it . . . This weekend, W. finished reading Cather's *One of Ours* aloud to me; we spoke of how deep an impression this novel makes on our souls. Afterwards, he went to the college library and checked out Wharton's *Son at the Front*; last night, he read the first chapter to me. War, war, war . . . I am adrift as I can never remember having been – vampirized of my heart's blood by awareness of what Matthew Arnold well called this "meadow of calamity," this "darkling plain." Wordless, almost –

I am a hopeless case, old compañero – ever gnawing on my own heart. The news is unbearable. Every day, unbearable.

Congress voted against setting a timetable to withdraw from Iraq. Juvenal wrote, "The depths of depravity are not reached in one day."

Bloomed by Harold Bloom's book! Stray wisps of Gnostic ideas darting in and out of my mind. Just read a review of the new book on the Gospel of Judas. Need time to re-arrange all this inside that windswept place where the brain resides.

No heart to talk with you about the continuing crashing of this society, old compañero.

I hope fervently I won't discover I'm a Gnostic! Am still reading W's cousin's grandmother's odyssey from Bavaria to Jerusalem to Cuba to the U.S. as though I myself am living it, that is how raptly I've been reading it. Perhaps there is no other "world" or "realm" such as the one I visited in last night's dream. But whatever hook or crook or grace, we human beings were given the redeeming gift of imagination – that is what fired the words of that art song I recited to my beloved in my dream, and that is what lighted my way to recognize whose presence I sense during this last season of my life.

W. read to me Azorín's words in praise of how nobly his uncle lived with the affliction of old age, and the words the writer quoted from St. Theresa's *Camine de Perfection*, advising young postulants never to indulge in self-pity. A very eloquent passage. Listening, it came to me in a flash what I learned from my mother that was for me one of her greatest lessons. Forbearance. Stoicism. Acceptance of physical afflictions. Now I strive to live with forbearance, stoicism, acceptance of afflictions of the spirit too.

Finished reading Cooley's *The Archivist* with relief, but afterwards, the currents of thought stirred by it swirled in my head. I used to think I was batter than W. at keeping the outer world from inundating my inner world, but now I think the opposite: I think he knows better than I do how to keep it at some remove, lest it become a drowning pool. I realize that's what my "Palatine" trilogy is all "about."

As our car turned west on Mulberry Street, a sudden and violent torrent of rain. Just as suddenly it stopped. And I saw a cloud-figure in the blue-and-grey brooding skies, lifting his arm, leading his errant flock onward. It was Moses. ♣

2007

Spider Mother

I've always been fascinated by crawly things – lizards, insects, fishing worms – and spiders – and they've often found their way into my writing. The world outside my window and in my garden mirrors in many ways my relationship with my loved ones; when I watched this tiny spider through its short lifespan, and when I offered those images to my journal, this spider's story blossomed into the story of my mother, her small trials and triumphs. Aspects of our relationship came clear to me in ways that would have been impossible, had I never written the story of the spider.

Mary O'Dell

Surely she came from elsewhere, some field or corner lot where she found herself a wriggling dot, having hatched from her mother's eggball on some misty morning, here now in this tiny square room behind the toilet, suspended, silent and still in a dusty web, undisturbed by mop or broom. I move her with a gentle breath that causes her legs to draw in the slightest bit. And I wonder how long she's been here in this room. I should have captured her sooner, sooner. I should have stopped what I was doing and put her on a piece of paper and taken her to the door and sent her, with a puff of my breath, sailing into the weeds. But now she's gotten away. But maybe if I go and look, she'll still be there.

In the moon of bright December – good line from someone else's poem – I dream my mother alive and well as a small black spider, her web an invisible shred netting the space between wall and toilet tank. Beneath a dusty plunger stuck to the floor by a stasis of years. She is silent there, my mother, as spiders are, and she moves not at all. I know she lives only by her miniscule flexing when I breathe upon the web, she is noble there, my mother, keeping her place, snagging the errant, pesky gnat, the motes that settle. I torment her again with my breath and she moves, holds still, and I wonder if this speck of spider hatched in this very cubicle or was carried here on someone's cuff.

My mother came here, to her final resting place, from Redcar, England, by way of West Virginia, but at the last, as her body was sunk into Kentucky clay, it made no difference.

I touch the spider's web and am rewarded with a twitch, a sucking in of legs, and wonder how long spiders live and what it must be like to know all that, only what a spider knows.

My granddaughter saw a small house spider in my white enamel tub and fled the bathroom, locking the door behind her. I looked away and smiled. Fear is fear, after all, and she's never questioned mine for her. My mother's fears, which I found enormous and irrational, I tried to no avail to talk her out of. Mother, I'd say, what's the worst that can happen? Then I found out some of them had, and I was humbled. The rape when she was thirteen. By a friend of her father's, no less. In a chicken yard, no less. And her own mother so fearful of what people would think, forbidding her to ever mention it again.

I finally leave the stall, leave the still black dot in her web with not a further glance. Days later, I am haunted. It is as if a web of gray has formed behind my eyes, and in its center a speck of black waiting silent and still, its little legs drawn in, and even my breath doesn't make it move. ♣

2008

This Darkness

I have always kept a written journal of one kind or another: a diary when I was a pig-tailed girl, a mother's journey when I was pregnant with my son, a dream journal, a spiritual journal – a record of my life here on earth. But it wasn't until a special friend introduced me to the creative journal that I discovered a place to find and express myself as an artist. The journaling that I do now is more than recording life events, it is a spiritual alchemy: taking those things that have happened, the joy and the suffering, the sorrow and the fear and transforming those things into something else. Something beautiful. Into gold.

Christine Lincoln

SEPTEMBER 14

Tonight I decided to take my walk in utter darkness. I loved it. There is something delicious in being completely surrounded by blackness. One by one I turned off all the lights except the brightest. I waited until I was standing near the middle of the room before switching off the last and brightest lamp, throwing the room into darkness before my eyes had time to adjust. It was so black I could see nothing, not even my own body, and even though I know this house as intimately as I know the lines on the palms of my hands, I was instantly disoriented. In the darkness possibilities grow. Where before, I was surrounded by the familiar, I am thrown into a place where someone could be lurking in the corner of the room waiting to pounce. The floor could have caved in without my knowing it; if I take a step forward I might fall to my death to the basement floor. In the darkness fear fills me. It starts in my belly like tendrils of some living thing, growing, spreading into the tops of my legs. I am rooted to this place where I know I am safe, unmoving in the darkness. And instantly I am taken back to my childhood. Playing hide-and-go-seek in the dark of night on Radnor Ave. The thrill of being caught, or of not being caught if your hiding place was good enough. The thrill and foreboding of being all alone in the middle of the night and perhaps no one will find me. But I was found or either turned myself in. So I move. I slide forward, careful. I move slowly because I cannot see myself. I have disappeared and I am not sure that I am real. And then something happens. The same darkness that at first frightened me now begins to comfort me. It offers me its freedom. It tells me that I am free here in the darkness because I am hidden. I am vulnerable and yet I am concealed. I can tell when I leave the living room because the carpet drops off beneath my shoes and I am walking on hardwood floor. Still slowly through this river of darkness. My footfalls against the hardwood sound like the beating of a heart. Da-dump, Da-dump, Da-dump. A heart beating in the darkness. The darkness is a womb. This darkness is an amnion. It is a place of unlimited potential, an incubator of ideas. The place of fear, yes, but also imagination and creativity. A place of protection and freedom and life. **This darkness is an amnion.** ⚘

Contributors

DIANA ANHALT (MEXICO) is a former teacher, newsletter editor and book reviewer for *The Texas Observer*. She is the author of *A Gathering of Fugitives: American Political Expatriates in Mexico 1948-1965* (Archer Books), also translated into Spanish. Her short stories, poetry and essays have been published in Mexico and the United States.

DEBORAH ARNOLD (MD) worked as a medical editor in Philadelphia before stumbling on nearby Historic Rittenhouse, where she learned papermaking, a passion that she turned into a business, Galaxy Papers. Deborah teaches collage, papermaking and book arts at community art centers. This is her first published work.

RUTH BEKER (ISRAEL) is a poet, photographer and journalist. Her poems have appeared in *Voices Within the Ark: The Modern Jewish Poets; Without a Single Answer: Poems on Contemporary Israel;* and *Unsettled: An Anthropology of the Jews.*

AUDREY BORENSTEIN (NY) is co-founder of The Life Writing Connection, which preserves privately-held, unpublished life writings by 20th century Americans. Her journal writings have appeared most recently in *In Pieces: An Anthology of Fragmentary Writing.*

VICKI BROADRICK (CA) spent her career as an elementary school teacher, stained glass artist, and therapist. She has kept a journal since she was ten years old. She lives in the San Bernardino mountains where her great grandparents, Maggie and Will Van Slyke, ended their cross country trek in the late 1860s.

LEE WARNER BROOKS (MI) has been a Yellow Cab driver in Ann Arbor, an editor and writer for publishers in Pennsylvania and Maryland, an editor of the *Michigan Law Review*, a law clerk for a federal appellate judge, and a partner in the litigation department of the law firm of Honigman Miller Schwartz and Cohn in Detroit. His book of sonnets, *Novlets*, will be published in 2009.

SAUCI CHURCHILL (MD) taught high school, worked as a law librarian for many years in the inner core of a government building, and now works in a garden, at the Hillwood Museum and Garden. Her publishing credits include, among others, *Quartets, Bitterroot, Poet Lore* and *Washington Review*. She is author of two poetry chapbooks, *Running Down Division Street* and *A Red Fin.*

SALLY PEARSON CONGLETON (KY) lives in a 100-year-old house on a farm in Kentucky with her husband of 55 years, two rescued dogs and a herd of Appaloosa horses. This is her first publication.

ORMAN DAY (NC) is writing a book about his backpacking journeys in 90 countries and the 50 states. His last adventure: at age 56, he canoed the Mississippi from Minneapolis to New Orleans, a two-month voyage during which he was nicknamed "Old Man River."

DONNA EMERSON (**CA**) is a college teacher, social worker, photographer and writer. Her poems have appeared in *California Quarterly, Big Scream, Chicago Quarterly Review,* among others.

SINDEE ERNST (**MD**) is an Integrative Breathing Practitioner and a computer teacher. Her work has appeared in *Passager, Urbanite, Tiny Lights* and *Brainchild.*

MICHAEL ESTABROOK (**MA**) is the author of 16 poetry chapbooks, most recently, *methinks I see my father.* He has a PhD in History and Genealogy from Warnborough University in London.

SIMKI GHEBREMICHAEL (**MD**) has bounced back and forth between her native California and Washington DC since high school. Her first husband was from Eritrea and they have two daughters, one living in Berkeley and one in Prague. Integrating cross-cultural identities is the focus of her writing. She works as an editor and will receive her MFA from American University at age 58.

STEPHANIE GRAHAM (**MD**) has had her photographs about urban ecology featured in *Baltimore Magazine, Baltimore Sun, Baltimore City Paper, The Amicus Journal, NYC,* and elsewhere. Her photographs appear on CD covers for The Preservation Hall Jazz Band.

WENDY HOFFMAN (**MD**) has done performance art and given multi media art exhibits in Chicago, New York, and on tour. She now lives in Baltimore where she works as a psychotherapist and writes poetry and short stories.

BILL HOFFMANN (**MN**) was a pilot in Viet Nam, resigned in '74, traveled the country in a converted bread van, did oil field work in Africa and Papua New Guinea, returned to Sudan as manager of a famine relief project in Darfur, and spent ten years in a sawmill in Washington, till he quit the mill to care for his father.

FEDORA HOROWITZ (**FL**) was the Artistic Director of The Lyric Chamber Ensemble in Detroit, and for 20 years her musical career did not allow time for writing. In 2000 she moved to Florida and joined a writers' group. She was a 4-time winner of the Sylvia Wolens Jewish Heritage Competition and has had several stories published in *Passager.* She is at work on her first novel, *A New Life,* about the love between a young Jewish girl and a Muslim man in 1940s Palestine.

GLORIA DeVIDAS KIRCHHEIMER (**NY**) is the author of a short story collection, *Goodbye, Evil Eye,* and co-author of *We Were So Beloved,* a nonfiction book.

KENDRA KOPELKE (**MD**) is a writer, editor and publisher. She directs the MFA in Creative Writing & Publishing Arts at the University of Baltimore

Contributors

and is founding co-editor of *Passager*, now in its 19th year. She has published four books of poems.

KATHLEEN MARIE LEARY (FL) retired from radio operations and production in Kentucky, and moved to the Gulf Coast of Florida to become an artist.

CHRISTINE LINCOLN (PA) is the author of *Sap Rising*, a novel written in stories. She was the first author to represent the U.S. in South Africa's Year of the Writer Celebration. Christine has appeared on NPR, *The Oprah Winfrey Show*, and has been featured as a "Phenomenal Woman" in *O: The Oprah Magazine*. She is the founder of A Woman's Word Production, a company whose vision is to help women exercise their right to speak: to find and develop their voices and manifest healing through the telling of their stories.

TERRY MILLER (NY) retired from the faculty of Kingsborough Community College and continues to read and write, the latter courtesy of the Andrew Heiskell Library of Talking Books for the visually impaired. She lives with her husband of 69 years.

LALITA NORONHA (MD) is a research scientist, science teacher, poet, writer and editor. Her short story collection, *Where Monsoons Cry*, was published in 2004. She is a fiction editor for *The Baltimore Review*.

MARY O'DELL (KY) is the author of *A Dangerous Man*, a chapbook of poems. She is founder and president of Green River Writers, Inc. in Louisville, Kentucky.

RICHARD PEABODY (DC) founded *Gargoyle Magazine* back before Elvis died. Issue #54 just appeared. Some of his titles include: *Conversations with Gore Vidal; Mondo Barbie; A Different Beat: Writings by Women of the Beat Generation; Coming to Terms: A Literary Response to Abortion;* and *Kiss the Sky: Fiction & Poetry Starring Jimi Hendrix.*

ROSALIE SANARA PETROUSKE (MI) has published poems in *The Seattle Review, Passages North,* and *The Red Rock Review,* among others. Her essays have appeared in *American Nature Writing: A Sierra Club Anthology.*

MARY PRATT (VT) has been a technician in a geology lab, a teacher, a clergywoman and an apple picker. She performs with Quatrain, a spoken word quartet.

DIANA RAAB (CA) is the author of seven books of nonfiction and poetry, including, *Healing with Words,* forthcoming in 2010. Her memoir, *Regina's Closet: Finding My Grandmother's Secret Journal,* won the 2008 National Indie Excellence Award for Memoir and the 2009 Mom's Choice Award for Adult Nonfiction. www.dianaraab.com.

LIZ RHODEBECK (WI) is a community news columnist and feature contributor for Lake Country Publications. She has published two chapbooks, *Benthos* and *The Book of Ruth*. www.waterwriter.com.

JAMES SEDWICK (NY) is a poet, photographer and mental health counselor for children and families in a public school health clinic.

LOUISE ROBERTS SHELDON (MD) was a reporter for *LIFE* and an editor of *Smithsonian Magazine*, as well as a correspondent for UPI, *The Christian Science Monitor*, and *The Middle East*. She is author of a collection of nonfiction stories, *Casablanca Notebook*, and a novel, *Wind in the Sahara*.

WILLIAM STIMSON (TAIWAN) leads dream groups at various universities in Taiwan and, once a month, conducts a silent meditation retreat at a Buddhist temple on Taiwan's Bamboo Mountain. He spends his free time planting trees on an eroding mountain slope that he's trying to bring back to life.

PANTEA A. TOFANGCHI (MD) is an Iranian-American poet, writer and graphic designer. She is a graphic designer for *Passager*, teaches at the University of Baltimore, and writes poems (in English), essays, stories and plays (in Persian). She enjoys making hand-made books of her work. Her poems have appeared in *Welter* and *American Noir*.

Her Persian work has appeared in magazines and newspapers in Iran.

JANICE WILSON STRIDICK (NJ) is a writing teacher and editor. She is founder of Southbound Press which published *The View in Winter*, a book of her grandmother's poems illustrated by her mother.

MARY F. WHITESIDE (TX) was a teacher, an instructional designer and information architect. An avid reader and walker on the blackland prairies, she took her first writing class after she retired.

JENNIE L. WINTER (ID) retired from teaching English and art to live in Idaho on the old homestead where she grew up with her eight brothers. She is an artist, sculptor and writer with five children, ten grandchildren and four great grandchildren.

ANN ZAHN (MD) has taught etching, woodcut and design and, since 1977, runs the Printmakers Workshop in her studio. Her work is in many collections, including the Museum of Modern Art (NY), Museum of Modern Art (Buenos Aires), Corcoran Gallery of Art, and the National Museum of Women in the Arts.

IN LEGENDS, the crane stands for longevity, peace, harmony, good fortune and fidelity. A high flyer, it is cherished for its ability to see both heaven and earth. These ancient, magnificent birds, so crucial in the wild as an "umbrella species," are now endangered and must be protected.

Passager Books is dedicated to making public the passions of a generation vital to our survival. We invite you to help us carry out our mission.

ALSO FROM PASSAGER BOOKS

A Cartography of Peace
by Jean L. Connor

Improvise in the Amen Corner
by Larnell Custis Butler

The editors are delighted to present *Six over Sixty*, a series of chapbooks by writers whose work has appeared in *Passager*. These six limited-edition chapbooks will be available individually and as a set.

A Little Breast Music
by Shirley J. Brewer

A Hinge of Joy
by Jean L. Connor

PASSAGER JOURNAL publishes twice a year, once early in the new year and again in the summer. For subscription information and guidelines please visit our web site at www.passagerpress.com.

Keeping Time was designed and typeset by Pantea Amin Tofangchi using InDesign. The text pages are set in Adobe Garamond Pro and Gill Sans.

The cover image is a collage entitled "Writing through the Blues" created by Deborah Arnold.

The editors are grateful for the editorial support of Christina Gay and Lindsey Wittstruck. They also wish to thank all of the writers who sent excerpts from their journals.

The text papers are Woodlawn and Anthem Matte. Printed in 2009 by United Book Press, Inc. in Baltimore, Maryland.